CARP ON THE FLY

CARP ON THE FLY

A Flyfishing Guide

Barry Reynolds
Brad Befus
John Berryman

Foreword by Dave Whitlock

JOHNSON BOOKS
Boulder

SPRING CREEK PRESS
Estes Park

Published in the United States by Johnson Books, a division of Johnson Publishing Company, 1880 South 57th Court, Boulder, Colorado 80301.

9   8   7   6   5   4   3

Cover design: Bob Schram/Bookends
Cover illustration: Jay P. Snellgrove

Library of Congress Cataloging-in-Publication Data
Reynolds, Barry.
  Carp on the fly: a flyfishing guide / Barry Reynolds, Brad Befus,
John Berryman; foreword by Dave Whitlock.
        p.   cm.
  Includes index.
  ISBN 1-55566-207-2 (cloth: alk. paper).—ISBN 1-55566-186-6
(pbk.: alk. paper)
  1. Carp fishing.   2. Fly fishing.   I. Befus, Brad.   II. Berryman,
John.   III. Title.
SH691.C3R45   1997
799.1'7483—dc21   97-18257
                                                                CIP

Printed in the United States by
Johnson Printing
1880 South 57th Court
Boulder, Colorado 80301

Printed on recycled paper with soy ink

CONTENTS

Preface   vii

Foreword   ix

Introduction   xiii

Acknowledgments   xvii

1. Why Not?   1

2. About Carp   11

3. Locating Feeding Carp   31

4. What Carp Eat   53

5. Carp Flies   71

6. Presentation   107

7. Fly Tackle for Carp   127

8. Putting It Together   133

Appendix   147

Index   153

PREFACE

This is the third book on which Barry Reynolds and I have collaborated, and it is the first book in which the talented Brad Befus becomes a member of the team. I get older and slower while the folks I write with become younger and smarter. It seems sort of unfair.

On the other hand, in the course of working on this book, I had the opportunity to work with not one, but two, innovative, articulate, systematic, enthusiastic flyfishers. Their exhaustive knowledge of the subjects encompassed by this book made its preparation easy. Translating their boundless enthusiasm for those same topics to the printed page was a much more daunting task. I only hope that I managed it.

Of the three books, this one has been the most fun to write, by far. Challenging a few assumptions and crying out loudly when the emperor has no clothes is always fun for a writer. Pioneering a new topic, revealing the underpinnings for what the three of us hope will become a new, very important part of the sport of flyfishing is even more fun. In the course of all this, I hope we'll manage to convince you to devote a bit of time and energy to learning to flyfish for carp.

You may know that the first book Barry and I did together was about learning to flyfish for northern pike, a savage, tackle-busting, thrilling fish on a fly rod. Well, if you liked learning to flyfish for northern pike, you're gonna *love*—but for some very different reasons—learning to flyfish for carp!

John Berryman
Aurora, Colorado
May, 1997

FOREWORD

The subject of this book may very well be the last great frontier of opportunity for flyfishers across North America. Yet, if it were written ten years earlier, I doubt if it would have had any chance of acceptance in this sport. It will be accepted now, because each year flyfishing is becoming much more popular with people of all ages and occupations across the U.S. and Canada and also because there is a new generation of flyfishers who have had to open up their minds to alternative fishing due to the rising expense, crowding, and sometimes scarcity of the traditionally loved, quality trout, char, and salmon waters.

Growing up in Oklahoma, I was not born with a fly rod in my hand. But at nine, I received an old, used bamboo rod that my dad purchased for me at an Iowa pawn shop. As I grew up, I flyfished nearby warmwater ponds and creeks. They were loaded with all sorts of fish eager to eat my flies. I remember catching numerous carp on sunfish flies and a mulberry fly that I tied to match the annual spring mulberry fall along the bottom-land creeks of northeast Oklahoma. The carp always were the most colorful, biggest, and hardest fighting of any fish that I'd catch.

I was not told it was uncool to catch bass, sunfish, carp, drum, gar, and catfish on flies until I was a young adult and made my first pilgrimage to Montana's trout paradise. But, sadly, I was influenced by my trout-flyfishing role models and began to look down on the wonderful native fish of my childhood and I turned my back on them for about twenty years. Then I began to yearn to return to my flyfishing roots ... the warm waters of eastern Oklahoma and western Arkansas ... to retrace the fishing footsteps of my youth there.

I've had so much more excitement and pure fun from then until now, some thirty years later, by adding warmwater fish to my flyfishing experiences that if I had to make a choice between warm- and coldwater fish—I'd hate to choose—I really wouldn't hesitate a moment.

But I must admit, I stayed in the closet all those years about my interest in and love for flyfishing for carp. I did this out of concern for what it might do to my flyfishing "reputation." I'm happy to say that I no longer fear that and, in the last three or four years, I have been telling carpin' stories and encouraging flyfishers to sample them. As a matter of fact, almost always one or two of my listeners will "come out," too, with some carp adventures of their own.

Carp are such neat, magnificent fish. They have adapted to nearly every water system we have, from cold to tropical, and have maintained their numbers amidst nearly all forms of harvesting—commercial netting, Rotenone, bow hunting, snagging, and fishing. Most cultures in Europe and Asia highly respect and value carp, and it's time that we do, as well.

In my opinion, carp are a supreme fly-rod challenge, equal to or excelling selective trout, bonefish, or permit in difficulty to take on a fly. To be successful hooking carp on flies, one must be very skilled at fly selection, casting, presentation, and fighting fish. Over the last two years, my two best destination flyfishing trips have been to the pristine carping flats of Lake Michigan, where my wife Emily and I joined George von Schrader (author of *Carp are Gamefish, Too*) to pole for golden-clad monsters that averaged twenty pounds. When one of these big guys grabs your fly, it speeds off on several 200-yard or longer dashes (we even had to follow some of them with the boat) and gives an incredible battle for twenty or thirty minutes on seven- and eight-weight tackle. They tested us, they fascinated us, they amazed us, and they thrilled us.

I could go on and on with my unchecked enthusiasm about these fish, but it's time to let Barry and Brad take you forward into this last frontier of freshwater flyfishing. They are exceedingly well-tuned to every aspect that you'll need to know to discover the unique challenges and limitless pleasures that flyfishing for carp offers. With their help, you'll be able to discover a sport fish that will absolutely intrigue you ... and there are probably some carp just minutes from your home or office.

It's sort of like having virgin bonefish or permit flats right in your back yard!

Dave Whitlock

Note: Dave Whitlock's favorite carp flies appear in the Appendix.

INTRODUCTION

I can remember with great detail when I received my formal introduction to carp. I was fishing Elevenmile Reservoir in Colorado about six years ago. It was late June and the pike I'd come to catch had begun moving into deeper water. Fishing was generally slow and, as the day warmed, pike fishing in the shallows came to a virtual halt. At about noon, things picked up a bit as one of the damselfly hatches, for which the lake is famous, began to come off.

I shrugged my shoulders, stuck my huge size 3/0 Bunny Fly on my drying patch, and tied on a lighter tippet and an olive damselfly nymph. Moving over to the reservoir's inlet and casting my nymph, I picked up a seven-and-a-half-pound rainbow on my third or fourth cast. Perhaps the day would turn out all right, after all, I decided.

I worked my way around the inlet to a small bay where, even from a distance, I could see that things were happening. When I got closer, I was amazed at what I saw: literally hundreds, perhaps a thousand (no kidding) tails, intermittently waving above the surface of the water as carp, feeding in about a foot of water and tailing almost exactly like bonefish, cashed-in on the damselfly bonanza.

Halfheartedly, knowing that carp didn't take flies, I cast the nymph at one group of feeding carp. A carp promptly moved over to my fly, tailed for a moment, and swam off.

I repeated this fruitless procedure perhaps half a dozen times before a thought occurred to me. Was it possible that the carp were gently mouthing my fly and spitting it out before I could feel them?

I cast again, and once more a large carp swam over to my fly. Its snout dipped, its tail came up, but this time I gently tightened the line. There was weight there! The instant I felt the weight, I set the hook.

While I'm not sure exactly what happened next, I am sure that it happened very fast. At the conclusion of that confusing series of events, I was left standing with a slack line, no fly, and a dumb look on my face. But I had figured out at least one way to catch a carp on a fly. I had a ball for the rest of the day. I even landed a few carp. That was my first carp lesson.

As time passed, I had other, wonderful carp-days, and experimentation produced new tactics. My growing affection for the fish was measured by the fact that I never seemed to have enough of those carp-days. I was quietly, secretly, turning into a carp-freak, but I managed to keep my deviant behavior to myself.

At about this time, I met an angler named Brad Befus. He was a young flyfishing fanatic who managed to keep body and soul together by working at Front Range Anglers in Boulder, Colorado. He and a partner now own the store.

Although still under thirty years of age, Brad had managed to fish the world over, in fresh- and saltwater. A few trips with Brad convinced me that he was a terrifically adaptable flyfisher. I think adaptable means, among other things, the ability to maximize every opportunity. Adaptable flyfishers can become great, all-around anglers, and Brad emphatically is a great, all-around angler. He can also cast. I won't say how far or how accurately. I will say that you can always tell when he's given a demonstration at an outdoor show by the look of anglers as they walk away from the casting pool, white-faced, their jaws hanging, shaking their heads in disbelief.

On a slow day, while Brad and I were telling lies in lieu of catching fish, he allowed as how he'd been known to cast to a carp upon occasion—just for fun. It wasn't a serious thing, of course.

I admitted to the same and casually suggested that I might know where a fellow could catch a carp—purely for grins, naturally. In case the bass weren't biting, you know. Brad then mentioned that he happened to know of a place where, if one didn't mind slumming a bit, one could catch a thirty-pound carp as a break from fly-fishing for northerns.

I expressed mild interest in seeing such a place, and after Brad pried my hands from his throat, we agreed that we should go there. Right then.

That trip marked the real beginning of this book. For the next three years, Brad and I fished each other's prime carp waters, showed each other the tactics we'd developed individually, and evolved strategies and tactics together that worked far better than anything we'd done separately.

We developed variations on Bob Clouser's deadly Clouser's Swimming Nymph that, for whatever reason, work very well on carp. We learned that carp will, if the opportunity presents itself, forage for living prey as aggressively, and nearly as effectively, as any game fish. To our surprise, we even succeeded in getting carp to take imitations of adult damsels.

I think it's probably true that the instinctive reaction that causes a flyfisher to cast to a moving fish is even stronger than the instinctive reaction that prompts a fish to strike at a fly. In the case of carp, however, many anglers have fallen prey to a collection of preconceptions, half-truths, and outright lies that have prevented them from even casting to carp. And rarely does an angler who deigns to cast to carp do so with any real commitment.

The result is that anglers who don't cast to carp—and that's the vast majority of them—are missing out on one helluva lot of fun. A sadder situation exists among those few anglers who do cast to carp but do so without the same level of intensity that they bring to fishing for other species. They have come so close, yet they are so far away.

Brad and I think it's time that situation changed. We're going public with our carp-madness, and we're hoping we can convince you to come along on what we promise will be an interesting journey. After you've caught your first carp and you've finished shaking, we ask but one thing of you—spread the word!

Barry Reynolds
Aurora, Colorado
May, 1997

ACKNOWLEDGMENTS

The most pleasant part of writing this book was the opportunity it gave Barry, Brad, and me to work with old friends again and to make new ones. Though we're sure to miss a few people who deserve recognition, we want to thank those who contributed most directly to this book.

Dave Whitlock generously took time from his busy schedule to read the book, write a foreword, and add his favorite carp flies. Len, Darrel, and Dave of The Trout Fisher in Denver provided help and encouragement, as did Brad's staff at Front Range Anglers in Boulder. Art Scheck and John Likakis helped us find Chuck Tryon, who came through with crucial reference materials. Thanks to John Barr for his help. We also want to thank editors Scott and Julie Roederer of Spring Creek Press and the staff at Johnson Books for their continued support of our work.

Others contributed in less tangible, but just as important, ways. Thanks to Susan, Chrissy, and Mike Reynolds, Lisa Befus, Judy Miller, Jill, Dr. Marvin Luttges, Al Marlowe, Mom, and Wally Bupp.

To all, our deepest thanks.

Barry Reynolds
Brad Befus
John Berryman

ONE

WHY NOT?

Yes, this really is a book about flyfishing for carp. We're absolutely serious about this and we hope you are equally serious about learning to flyfish for what is certainly the last, great, underfished, overlooked flyfishing resource in North America. But why are carp overlooked? If carp are such wonderful quarry, why don't more people fish for them? Well, we have some ideas about that. See if this sounds familiar.

You're fishing a lake with your buddy when he suddenly sets the hook. In an instant, all hell breaks loose. His reel starts shrieking and so does he. Soon his line is only a memory and he's deep into his backing. Still yelling like a maniac, he's forced to run up and down the bank, slipping and sliding, more in the water than out of it, and all you can do to help is get out of his way.

You get your camera ready. Whatever it is, it's one terrific fish, and frankly you're more than a little jealous. It could be a really big northern, but this fish has already shown more endurance than most northerns do. Maybe it's a largemouth—but if it is, it's a clear-cut, no-kidding, world-record fish. Excitement mounts as, after two or three more blistering runs, your buddy manages to winch the brute nearer to shore.

As the fish gets closer, you see a vague shadow in the water and you begin to get a sense of the size of the fish. Lord, but it *is* big! Its thrashing stirs up the silt and it's tough to see the fish, but it's tiring and your friend brings it closer. Then there's a glimpse of a

Lord, it was big! Then there was a glimpse of a tail and a bronze flash. (Brad Befus)

tail, a bronze flash as the sun hits the fish's large, coarse scales, and finally you get a look at those unmistakable lips.

The laughter starts.

Shooting faster than John Wayne in *The Sands of Iwo Jima*, you hold the button down on your camera—you'll never let your friend forget this! The look on the guy's face—it's priceless! From boundless joy to deepest depression in a heartbeat. You're laughing so hard you can hardly keep the camera on your friend; and as for your friend, well, let's just say that his language leaves something to be desired.

Your buddy finally lands the fish, but he refuses to be photographed with it. This, of course, doesn't stop you from continuing to snap pictures. If you have your way, those photos will appear on the bragging board of every fly shop in town. Finally, the carp is either released (with curses and a kick) or thrown on the bank to die.

What's wrong with this scene? Brad and I want to suggest to you that both the laughter at the angler and the disdain of the fish are misplaced.

Your friend didn't hook a puny fish. He caught a fish that thrilled him right down to the soles of his waders and tested every bit of his skill. He caught a big, strong fish that fought with no holds barred until it was netted (and if it was like most carp, it didn't stop then). And he caught a fish that is rarely caught on artificial lures of any kind and that is taken even more rarely on flies. Most significantly, he caught what he thought was the fish of a lifetime—until he saw it.

We suggest that he really did catch the fish of a lifetime, but due to a variety of unfortunate preconceptions, he simply didn't perceive it as such.

So why do so many anglers disdain carp? Why do they make fun of carp and the people who have the "misfortune" to catch one in the presence of witnesses?

We think one of the reasons is the carp's unfortunate designation as a trash fish. In the eyes of many anglers, fish that attain enough size to be of interest fall into just two categories, game fish (or sport fish) and trash fish. We're not exactly sure how a fish earns its designation. Trout and whitefish, for instance, are native to the same waters, have similar diets, and are taken readily by anglers. Yet, in the opinion of many anglers, the whitefish is a trash fish and is often heaved on the bank to die.

Carp may have made the trash fish list in part because of the kind of water they are sometimes found in. Yes, carp can live in water that is unsuitable for virtually any other fish. They're a tough, smart fish that can survive even man's pollution. But carp do equally well in pristine waters. Indeed, some of the country's finest trout, northern pike, bass, and walleye fisheries also support healthy populations of carp. And, in those clean, pure waters, the diets of carp can be as exclusive and above reproach as any trout's.

In Colorado's Elevenmile Reservoir, home to trout and pike of breathtaking size, carp also inhabit the waters. They take advantage of the reservoir's damselfly hatches, and wonderful fly-rod action for carp can be had. Sipping as delicately as any trout, we've also seen these carp smut midges from the surface. The word spooky doesn't begin to describe these surface-feeding fish. In the spring and early summer when populations of baitfish and young-of-the-year are high, we've even seen carp smash through schools of baitfish with all of the grim efficiency of marauding striped bass.

Whatever the reason, it is definitely man who put the "trash" in "trash fish."

There may be another reason carp have a bad reputation with flyfishers. We don't disdain carp just because they're a trash fish (as a matter of fact, they were deliberately stocked in the United States because they were desired by our ancestors); nor do we turn up our noses because they are sluggish fighters (they definitely are not). We may look down on carp because they can seem too challenging to catch with fly tackle and because a carp of any real size can be very difficult to land.

Brad and I had an occasion to observe some carp preconceptions in action during one of our casting clinics. As many instructors do, we had our students casting hookless pieces of yarn into our casting pool, which contained some small trout, bluegills, and carp. One of our students was a woman who had never fished before.

A carp of good size and respectable muscular development took a fancy to her piece of yarn and, holding the yarn firmly in its mouth, left for points unknown at a good clip. She yelled and tried to put the brakes on the fish. Since there was no hook to jab the fish, the carp saw no reason to let go or even pay much attention to her, and it hung on to the yarn stubbornly. Eventually, the woman proved more determined than the carp, and her yarn fly came sailing back at her.

She was thrilled beyond words! Not only had one of her first casts actually interested a fish, the fish it interested was one tough character that gave her all the tussle she wanted. Later that day, during the fishing portion of the class, the same woman hooked and landed a perfectly respectable eighteen-inch brown trout.

"Gee," she said, regarding her trout somewhat unhappily. "I think I liked catching the carp better."

You know what happened, don't you? Voices spoke up from every side, clamoring to be the first to tell her that the carp was a trash fish and that she should be much prouder of the trout.

At this point, we ask the following question. If she really should have been happier with the trout, why was it necessary for anyone to tell her so? After catching both a carp and a trout, shouldn't *she* have been able to make the decision about which fish was more fun to catch?

She did make that decision, but thanks to her peers espousing the virtues of game fish over trash fish, she is now well on her way to developing a conventional mentality and missing out on a lot of fun. Such a shame, for carp demand every bit of sophistication the flyfisher has at his or her disposal.

Question: Have you ever flyfished for carp?

Think back over the years. Remember days on the water when nothing much was happening except for the occasional glimpse of a tail or areas of muddied water where schools of carp were working. Did you ever casually flip whatever happened to be attached to your leader at those big, bronze fish?

You're not alone if you have. One of the things that make carp so appealing is that they're a terrific alternative fish. When the trout or bass aren't hitting due to temperature extremes or simple cussedness, it's likely that carp will still be feeding.

This doesn't make them easier to catch than other fish—carp are as smart and spooky as fish come. But it *is* true that they can be active at times when other fish are not. Because of their tremendous adaptability to temperature changes, carp are available to the angler essentially year-round. If there is open water, it's likely you'll have the opportunity to cast to feeding carp. Brad and I have caught carp eleven months out of the year in Colorado.

Another question. If you've fished for carp, have you ever caught one on a fly rod?

We're willing to make a bet with you. We're willing to bet that if you've tried to catch carp, you've cast to many more of them than you've caught and that, by the percentages, your success in flyfishing for carp has been much, much lower than for other fish. Even more telling, we're willing to bet that one reason you

Carp are available to the flyfisher year-round. (Robert Sweet)

don't cast to carp more often is quite simply that you aren't convinced they can be persuaded to take a fly at all.

Brad and I used to share that feeling. I started out with the
carp-as-trash-fish mentality. Trash fish eat trash, I reasoned, and
wouldn't be interested in my ever-so-delicate-and-beautiful flies.
Therefore, on those rare occasions when I did cast to a carp, I was
sloppy and simply cast whatever happened to be attached to my
tippet. After I started making careful presentations using flies that

imitated what carp were eating, my success rate went up dramatically. Amazing!

In the balance of this book, Brad and I are going to ask you to keep an open mind. We think that if we can convince you to put aside a few preconceptions, we can teach you to take carp on a fly often enough to make flyfishing for carp something you do on purpose.

We're going to ask you to hone your existing skills even further and concentrate just as much on learning to flyfish for carp as you would on learning to flyfish for any game fish—for no matter what our preconceptions are or the opinions of other anglers may be, carp *are* game fish. Once you catch one, you'll agree.

If you elect to undertake the carp challenge, you will spend much time fishing in shallow water, where carp feed very much like bonefish. It will be finicky, technical sight-fishing to individual tailers or stealthy blind-casting into muddy areas where carp are feeding. Overall, it will be just as demanding as flyfishing for bonefish in the Bahamas, but a lot less expensive. Those spooky carp in the shallows will spot you if you're clumsy with your presentation, and they'll disappear as fast as any flats-feeding bonefish.

If you find the fish and don't put them down, new challenges will be placed upon you. Above all, carp are smart. They are not easily fooled and respond best to the presentation of a fly that looks and behaves like a natural food item. Carp can be selective. In our opinion, they can be just as selective as any trout.

Unlike trout and most other fish, a carp is essentially omnivorous and is often literally surrounded by food. With such riches close to hand, a carp may not be willing to chase your fly very far, nor is it likely to tolerate having a fly suddenly arrive in front of its nose with a splash. Determining the size of and subsequently hitting what is a comparatively small window is crucial. Carp can also be extremely leader shy, and the shadow of a false cast can send an entire group scurrying for cover. If you're not an accurate caster now, you will be after flyfishing for carp!

It's easy to tell a recent convert to flyfishing for carp. (Brad Befus)

And what if you meet all of these challenges and actually suc-
ceed in hooking a sizable carp? That's when everything you've
ever learned about fighting a fish will be tested. Any carp is strong,
and big carp (over fifteen pounds) are really strong. Because they
are so leader shy, it's practically certain that your tippet will be
lighter than you'd like it to be.

A world-record carp weighs over fifty pounds, and it may be
that carp of that size are, to all intents and purposes, impossible
to catch on the 3X tippets that seem to be required to take them.
My largest fly-rod carp to date is a forty-two-inch, thirty-eight-
pound fish, and it was *strong*. Neither one of us is sure we could
handle a fifty-pound fish. However, both Brad and I would love
to find out, and the sooner, the better!

You'll soon quickly find out why we say it's easy to tell a recent
convert to flyfishing for carp. It's the angler with the broken tippet, the shaking hands, the staring eyes, and the excited stammer.

In carp, we have a fish that is strong, smart, spooky, and catchable
with fly tackle. But that's not all of the story.

Carp are extremely hardy and can withstand wide temperature variations. If the water is liquid and sufficiently free of pollutants so that it doesn't spontaneously combust or glow in the dark, the chances are that carp can live in it. Even in inner-city waters, very large, very powerful carp may be present.

Carp live almost everywhere in the United States and are widely distributed around the world, so terrific sport for big fish is available to everyone—without driving for hundreds of miles or spending thousands of dollars for a place on private water.

Most significantly, carp are overlooked by flyfishers. Brad and I think they're overlooked because of their trash fish status and because anglers simply don't know how to fish for them. We hope this book will help change both the esteem flyfishers hold for the fish and their ability to catch carp. If we're successful, we're certain that the status of carp will change quickly.

Some more mature anglers will remember back to the forties and fifties, when fishing for in-shore saltwater fish with light tackle and fly rods was first becoming a popular sport. Those anglers may also remember that writers of the time wrote disparagingly about a noisome, useless fish that they casually referred to as the "saltwater sucker."

Today, we call them bonefish and anglers speak of them with religious fervor. Brad and I are hopeful that if bonefish can beat their bad press, perhaps carp can, too. And when you think about it for a moment, there are some interesting parallels between carp and bonefish:

Both are usually bottom feeders.
Both feed heavily on shellfish.
Both are schooling fish.
Both tail when feeding in shallow water.
Both are wary and frighten easily.
Both usually aren't eaten and are caught and released.
Both require similar tactical approaches.

Anglers didn't appreciate the wonderful sport offered by bone-fish until they understood the fish. Perhaps, in the case of carp, lack of understanding is a significant factor in the way anglers feel about them. The next chapter will begin providing you with information that will help you form an appreciation of carp.

TWO

ABOUT CARP

In this chapter, Brad and I want to give you a basic understanding of our quarry. We will discuss two fish: the common carp (*Cyprinius carpio*) and the grass carp or white amur (*Ctenopharyngodon idella*). The common carp is widespread in the United States. It is the carp you're most likely to have seen and by far the one you are most likely to cast to.

The grass carp's distribution is much more limited and stocking them is, in fact, prohibited in many states. Grass carp are usually planted to control weed growth, and we include this fish because, if it's available, it provides fabulous sport. It's just as tough and scrappy as the common carp and it jumps! Avoiding irate groundskeepers and furious gardeners at the golf courses and parks where grass carp are likely to be found adds another dimension to the sport.

Common Carp

To understand carp, it's appropriate to start at the beginning, and in the case of carp, the story begins a very long time ago.

History

If there was such a thing as a space shuttle 240 million years ago and we were orbiting the Earth in it, we'd see a planet that looked very little like the one depicted on today's globes. Instead of the familiar continents, we'd see a single supercontinent called Pangea. At that point in time, most of the major fish species that we know today were already in existence, albeit in somewhat primitive forms.

A mere forty million years later, things were a lot different. Pangea had begun to break up. As a result of this breakup, a number of aquatic and terrestrial species became isolated as the continents we know today were formed. Carp probably evolved somewhere in western Asia and/or eastern Europe after the continents separated.

Common carp don't do well in brackish water and were not able to migrate, as other freshwater fish such as pike are presumed to have done, during the melting that followed later ice ages. Once the continents were separated by saltwater, the carp that lived in Europe and Asia were effectively isolated from the New World for the next eighty to 100 million years.

When man arrived on the scene and began to form the construct that, for better or worse, we call civilization, he learned to build cities, to farm, and to raise animals. One of those animals was probably the carp.

Since little written evidence survives from this time, the history of the spread of carp is somewhat conjectural. Written records from China make mention of the carp as early as 500 B.C., and carp were probably imported to Europe from China in the eleventh or twelfth century. The Romans may have spread carp aquaculture to Italy and Greece. During the middle ages, monasteries certainly raised carp and may have spread the knowledge required to farm-raise the fish. Carp were probably introduced to England in 1496 and to Ireland about the time Pilgrims arrived at Plymouth Rock.

Carp arrived in America under the official auspices of the United States Fish Commission in the late 1870s. At that time, what we now call sport fishing was an activity carried out by a few very wealthy or very eccentric individuals. To the rest of the country, the word "fish" was synonymous with the word "food."

Hundreds of thousands of pounds of native fish were being harvested annually by any means available.

As a further impact to the fisheries, the U.S. was expanding, both agriculturally and industrially. Entire forests were felled, increasing sediments in streams and rivers. Burgeoning industries, unhampered by the concept of pollution, happily poured their waste into every available watershed. Between human consumption and adverse environmental pressures, our native fish were in trouble.

These pressures prompted Professor S. F. Baird, from his office in the Fish Commission, to comment that:

> Sufficient attention has not been paid in the United States to
> the introduction of the European carp as a food fish, and yet
> it is quite safe to say that there is no other species that promises
> so great a return in limited waters. It has the preeminent
> advantage over such fish as the black bass, trout, grayling, and
> others in that it is a vegetable feeder, and although not disdaining
> animal matters, can thrive very well upon aquatic vegetation
> alone. On this account, it can be kept in tanks and small ponds,
> and a very much larger weight obtained than the case of other
> kinds indicated. It is on this account that its culture has been
> continued for centuries. (From *Carp in North America*,
> American Fisheries Society)

Adding force to Baird's arguments, the Commission was also under increasing pressure from Americans of European descent to make carp available in the U.S. As many as 2,000 such requests were received in 1880, after formal stocking of carp had already begun.

In 1877, as a result of the pressure, 345 carp (118 scaled carp and 227 mirror and leather carp) were imported from Germany and placed in Druid Hill Ponds in Baltimore. These fish were considered so valuable that the ponds were guarded. Stocking programs conducted over the next few years then spread the progeny of these carp across the country.

While this is the history of the official arrival of carp in the U.S., it's almost certain that carp were informally stocked years

Robustly built and laterally compressed, the common carp is the one you're most likely to cast to. (Barry Reynolds)

earlier. Captain Henry Robinson of New York is credited with importing carp in the 1830s, and Julius A. Poppe may have introduced carp to California as early as 1872.

No matter how they arrived, it is clear that carp did well. Within four years of initial stocking activities, carp were being caught commercially in the Illinois, Missouri, and Mississippi rivers and from Lake Erie. Within a couple of decades, millions of pounds of carp were being harvested annually. And the rest is history.

The Family Tree

The common carp is a member of the minnow family, the largest freshwater fish family, with some 1,500 named species. Apart from carp, members of the minnow family with which American anglers are probably most familiar are shiners and chubs. Like other minnows, the carp possesses coarse scales, pharyngeal (in the throat) teeth, and a "Weberian apparatus" (more on this later). Unlike other minnows, which have soft fins, the first ray of the carp's dorsal and anal fins are spined.

Range

Carp live in all of the lower forty-eight states, Hawaii, and Mexico. As we've seen, they're widespread in Europe, in most of Asia, and in the British Isles. The northern portions of the Scandinavian countries, Canada, and Asia are too cold for carp.

Much of the African continent appears to lack carp, although the largest carp on record, an eighty-three-and-a-half-pound monster, was caught near Pretoria, South Africa in 1963. Australia has few, if any, carp and New Zealand, New Guinea, and parts of southern Asia have no carp. In summary, common carp range throughout the temperate zones of the New World and of Europe and Asia from the British Isles to Japan.

Carp have been formally and informally stocked throughout this range. Carp are very adaptable and opportunistic, and it is probable that their range is continuing to expand due to stocking and the carp's ability to thrive in varied environments.

Appearance and Size

For the technically inclined, the carp is properly described as a robustly built, laterally compressed fish with a large, triangular head. The head can make up as much as a quarter of the overall length of the fish and it tapers abruptly to the mouth—the feature of the fish that anglers find most recognizable. There are no teeth in the mouth proper, chewing being managed by the pharyngeal teeth. Unlike most freshwater fish, carp actually do chew or crush hard food items.

The color of carp is extremely varied. The most common color scheme consists of an olive/bronze back that transitions gradually to a yellow or cream belly. Fins are often red. But wild carp can interbreed with domestic carp, such as the Koi often found in

The partially scaled mirror carp and the scaleless leather carp comprise a small portion of the population. (Barry Renolds)

ornamental ponds, as well as with goldfish; because of this, white, gold, black, striped, and even calico color variations exist.

Scale patterns likewise vary. While carp are generally fully scaled, partially scaled (mirror) and scaleless (leather) carp also exist, though they comprise a small portion of the population.

There are many tales about the ultimate ages and sizes carp can reach. Stories are told of carp living for hundreds of years. And anyone who lives near a large lake has probably heard vague accounts about a diver who found carp so big that he got back in the boat and refused to go down again.

Actually, the truth is impressive enough. Captive carp have been known to live nearly a half-century, and the record American carp is a fish weighing seventy-four pounds that was taken from Mississippi's Pelahatchie Lake in 1963. However, since today's anglers are not prone to weigh or brag about their carp catches, it's possible that larger carp have been taken.

In the wild, both the life expectancy and size of carp vary depending upon their environment. As with other fish, water temperature is a critical factor. Broadly speaking, carp living in warm water grow faster, grow to larger sizes, and probably have shorter life spans than carp in cooler waters.

No matter where they live, carp grow very fast when they're young. This frantic growth slows as carp begin to spawn, when significant energy must be devoted to producing eggs and milt. Man has also interfered with this picture. Hybrid strains of carp grow faster than wild strains, and mirror and leather carp are, inch-for-inch, heavier than the more typical carp.

Finally, there are indications that carp grow more slowly in areas where they are crowded, perhaps due to factors other than simple exhaustion of food resources. Some researchers have suggested that carp in areas of high population density may produce chemicals that slow the overall growth rate.

Habitat

Like any fish, carp have preferred habitats, but they are a tremendously adaptable fish. It's probably safe to say that the waters you fish are more likely to have carp in them than not, no matter what the nature of the water. Pristine mountain lakes and reeking industrial rivers can both support good carp populations.

Since carp eat plant and animal matter, they prefer areas where both are present—typically shallow, weedy areas with muddy or sandy bottoms where they can forage on plants, insects, and crustaceans. Access to cover is important. Sometimes, the ability to flee into very thick weed growth provides enough security for the carp. Without it, they often remain close to deep water.

Carp are considered hardy in part because of their ability to withstand a very wide temperature range. The following table shows how extensive that range is:

Temperature	Remarks
39° F	Carp begin active feeding.
41° F	Carp begin pre-spawn move to shallows.
61° F	Sustained temperatures below this point lethal to carp eggs.

Temperature	Remarks
63° F	Probable lower limit for spawning.
66° F	Optimal temperature for carp.
72° F	Metabolism increases rapidly.
75° F	Probable upper limit for spawning.
79° F	Sustained temperatures above this point lethal to carp eggs.
90° F	Metabolism at a high rate. Large amounts of food required.
97–106° F	Lethal temperature limit for carp.

In addition to its tolerance of temperature extremes, the ability to withstand low oxygen levels and high turbidity contribute to the carp's reputation for hardiness. While carp begin to experience difficulty breathing when oxygen levels fall to 4.5 ppm (parts per million) and feeding and growth begin to slow when oxygen levels drop to 3 ppm, the fish can actually survive on 2 ppm dissolved oxygen or less.

Carp are often found in areas of low oxygen, such as muddy backwaters where vegetation is rotting. So, as you might expect, carp are very tolerant of turbidity and they can exist in waters that are so cloudy that overall light penetration is limited and the productivity of the water is adversely affected.

Senses

The ability to survive in turbid waters has placed some demands on carp in terms of their ability to perceive the world around them—principally to find food and avoid predators. Their senses have evolved to address these needs. Though carp possess good vision, they also depend upon their sense of hearing, smell, and taste. Anglers who understand how carp use their senses can learn some important lessons on how to catch carp.

Scientists have determined that many members of the minnow family have excellent color vision and that some species can see both infrared and ultraviolet portions of the spectrum, as well as perceive polarized light. Carp probably also have good visual acuity.

In waters where aquatic insects are present, carp feed heavily on both nymphs and emerging insects. Nymphs and other swimming insects are captured as the carp roots around on the bottom, and anyone who has cast a nymph to a carp can tell you that sight definitely plays a role in the carp's ability to feed on insects.

As far as surface feeding is concerned, Brad and I feel that, although carp may initially locate surface prey by sound, the actual capture of the prey is a function of vision. And, for what it's worth, we have also noted that carp appear to have a clear preference for flies colored in shades of tan/rust/brown, green/olive, and black/gray, further convincing us that visual cues are important to feeding carp.

As confirmation of how important vision is to carp, we've also seen carp flee the moving shadow made by a fly line in the air, scatter at the sudden movement of an angler, and run for the nearest cover when a camera lens or watch crystal catches the light.

Lesson #1: Carp can see quite well, certainly well enough to see your fly, very probably well enough to see you. Move slowly and cast carefully.

A carp has ears much like those present in other fish and, like other fish, a carp hears quite well. But that is only part of the story. Remember the "Weberian apparatus" mentioned earlier?

The Weberian apparatus is an assembly of bones and ligaments that connects the swim bladder of the carp with its inner ear. In effect, the swim bladder becomes a resonator and amplifier of sounds. The net effect is that a carp can hear much better and can hear a wider range of sounds than many other fish.

Like other fish, the carp possesses a lateral line—a series of nerve endings used to detect low frequency vibrations. The carp can use this sense to locate struggling prey, just as other fish do. But in the case of carp, it does more.

Unlike most of the other game fish that anglers pursue, carp are a social fish. It is likely that the lateral line sense also helps a carp remain in close contact with its school or shoal mates. In addition, it may also permit the carp to quickly respond to panic or fright from other members of the school.

Lesson #2: Wade very, very quietly.

As befits a fish that may forage in turbid waters or clouds of mud of its own making, the carp has a very well developed sense of smell. Water is routed through a pair of nostrils (properly called the nares) to receptors in the nasal cavity where smells are interpreted. Some experiments have suggested that a carp may be able to locate food items entirely by smell.

The carp's sense of smell may also serve as a warning device. Some other minnows, and perhaps carp, have large cells located in the skin that release chemicals known as pheromones when the surface of the skin is damaged. When other minnows smell these pheromones (also known as schreckstoff or "alarm substance"), the school scatters and runs for cover.

Lesson #3: A carp handled improperly or carelessly may emit a warning that will frighten off every other carp in the vicinity. Handle carp carefully!

Carp have a well-developed sense of taste equal to that of many higher animals. Experiments have established that carp can tell the difference between salty, bitter, and sweet tastes just as humans can. In addition, they appear to be sensitive to fish tastes extracted from skin and tissues. Many bait anglers believe that carp prefer the taste of things such as meat (fresh or spoiled), vanilla, cinnamon, corn, sweets (e.g., marshmallows, molasses, honey), and cheese.

There is reason to believe that if you like the smell or taste of something, a carp would like it, too. And if you would find the taste or smell of something to be offensive, a carp would, too.

Unlike humans, carp have taste buds located over the entire surface of their bodies. So, as a carp swims, it literally tastes the water through which it moves. It is likely that these taste buds help the carp find food that it may bump into in turbid waters. The barbels located at the edges of a carp's lips may also play a role in its sense of taste. Researchers believe that the carp's method of feeding created a need for enhanced sensory systems, because the fish's vision is so limited while bottom feeding. The barbels may function as a rather crude, initial food prospecting system as carp root around in bottom sediments.

Lesson #4: Avoid the use of products with offensive tastes and smells, such as bug dope, line dressing, fly floatants, gasoline, motor oil, and suntan lotion (except maybe coconut oil formulas).

Reproduction and Spawning

Among fish, there are several basic reproductive strategies. Some fish, such as guppies, bear relatively few, but well-developed, live young that are better equipped for survival than larval fish. Trout and other species lay eggs and conceal them from predators. Bass and panfish lay eggs and ensure their survival by guarding them and the newly hatched young. Still other fish, such as pike, walleye, and carp, lay many, many eggs, and even if most are eaten or destroyed, enough young reach adulthood to ensure species survival.

Carp are spring spawners. While they may begin moving into shallow areas when water temperatures reach the high thirties, spawning occurs at temperatures of sixty-three to seventy-five degrees. In North America, spawning season may begin as early as March in the southern U.S. and as late as mid-August in parts of Canada. To complicate the issue, carp have been known to spawn twice in a season, though the female lays fewer eggs the second time. Favored spawning areas may be used every year.

The ages of sexually mature carp vary due to the fact that sexual maturity is more dependent on the size of the carp than its age. Males usually begin to spawn when they are twelve inches long (at about two years old), and females when they are seventeen inches long (at about three years old). In areas where carp grow rapidly, males may spawn at one year of age; and in areas where carp grow slowly, females may not spawn until the age of five.

Carp aren't shy about spawning nor do they care if it is day or night. They spawn in one to two feet of water, accompanied by much splashing. Typically one male, but sometimes several, will pursue a female as she releases eggs and milt. During this process, a fifteen- to twenty-pound female carp may release more than two million eggs! The eggs are adhesive and stick to plants, submerged deadfall, and the bottom. In prime spawning areas, as many as 2,500 eggs per square yard of bottom have been reported.

With the water temperature at sixty-three degrees, the eggs hatch in about six days. After they hatch, the larva, born with a yolk sack and little resembling adult carp, attach themselves to vegetation and absorb the yolk sack over a period of several days. Then they begin to forage for algae and other very small organisms, and early growth is rapid. A young carp begins to look like a carp by the time it is about half-an-inch long, and the distinctive barbels are soon present. By the time a carp is one inch long, scales have begun to form and the fins have assumed roughly adult shapes.

Odd as it may sound given the sheer numbers of carp that hatch, it's possible that you've never seen a young one. They spend much of their early life buried in mud or sand. Rapid growth ends this behavior quickly. With good conditions, a carp that was a larva in March can be four to eight inches long in October. Hybrid carp may achieve even more impressive growth rates. Farm-raised carp in Israel—admittedly eating very well—can weigh as much as two pounds at the end of their first year.

Diet

In Chapter 4, we'll focus in some detail on what carp eat, but it's appropriate to comment briefly on the diet of carp at this point.

Feeding occurs throughout the day, and carp typically feed in water ranging from very shallow to perhaps ten feet in depth. Within this ten-foot column, carp will feed anywhere, depending on food availability. They will happily root around on the bottom, but they also feed successfully on suspended plankton and floating insects and seeds.

A rooting carp can penetrate five inches into soft bottom sediments, coming up with a mouthful of mud, which is then expelled from the mouth and gills, permitting the carp to pick out the food items. This behavior can be easily observed in common goldfish, as they routinely mouth and spit out fish food before finally ingesting it. The carp's gill-rakers provide additional food-filtering capability.

While small food items may be swallowed whole, larger bits or hard items are crushed by the pharyngeal teeth. The pharyngeal jaw, located almost directly behind the fish's gill-plate, is used to crush food against a chewing pad located roughly where a human's soft palate is found.

Young, fast-growing carp need food with enough calories to support their rapid growth, and animal food thus makes up the predominant portion of a young carp's diet. As you might expect, insect larvae, small crustaceans, and mollusks are favored food items.

As a carp grows, it becomes a true omnivore, eating living plants, animal life, and what is delicately referred to as "organic debris." Contrary to what many anglers believe, fish and fish eggs are rarely found in the digestive tracts of carp. What is often found inside carp is mud. Despite their attempts to strain food from silt, inevitably a certain amount of silt is consumed.

The relative amounts of plant, animal, and "debris" food items consumed by mature carp are a function of what is available to the fish, and many observers believe much of the live-plant portion of a common carp's diet may be consumed accidentally, a byproduct of the fish's foraging for insects. Because carp are such efficient feeders, fertile lakes can support huge numbers—as much as half a ton of carp per acre of lake.

Shoaling and Social Behavior

Carp are somewhat unusual in that they travel in groups, while most of the flyfisher's traditional quarry tend to be more solitary. While anglers often refer to any group of fish as a school, this is not technically correct. A school of fish is a group of fish that are swimming in a synchronized manner. Many small fish and fry travel in schools, responding together and almost instantly to a potential threat.

A shoal of fish is a group of fish that is formed by virtue of social interactions, such as group feeding or protection from predators. Most of the time when carp are traveling together and especially when they are of interest to the flyfisher, they are shoaling.

It's likely that communication within a shoal of carp occurs on several different levels. Their lateral line receives vibrations produced by other shoal-mates. This information helps a carp remain in close touch with the shoal and lets it know when other members of the shoal have been frightened or startled. In clear water, vision probably also helps a carp remain with the rest of the shoal.

The role of pheremomes or schreckstoff in communicating alarm to a shoal of carp has been mentioned above. When a shoal is alarmed, it may respond by ceasing to feed, by shoaling more tightly, or by leaving the area. Apparently this response is quite strong, for in experiments, other similar fish avoided a regularly-used feeding station after schreckstoff was released in the water.

Although carp hear extremely well, sound has, so far, not been found to play a role in shoal formation or in communication within a shoal.

Shoaling provides carp with several benefits. In laboratory experiments, it's been found that shoaling fish locate food more quickly and forage longer than individual fish. There even appears to be a visual-communication component to this. When one member of a shoal lowers its head to feed, other members begin to imitate it, as if the head-lowering provides a there's-food-around-here signal. In addition, shoaling fish have been observed to respond to the presence of a predator more rapidly than do individual fish, and the larger the shoal, the faster the response. Because they travel in shoals, carp respond to an angler's presence more quickly than do other fish and that response is likely to affect a larger group of fish.

The grass carp is a more elegant fish than the common carp. (Brad Befus)

Grass Carp

The grass carp is also an immigrant to our shores, though a much more recent one. Grass carp share many characteristics of common carp, but there are significant differences between them.

History

The grass carp seems to have originated in eastern China and Russia and has since become a world citizen. Beginning with the first formal records of grass carp stocking in Japan in 1878, the grass carp has subsequently been introduced into at least fifty countries, including the U.S. and Mexico. They appear to be breeding successfully in Mexico and Panama. Worldwide, grass carp live in much of Europe, Asia, and Africa.

Grass carp are raised for food and ornamental purposes. In addition, grass carp can be almost entirely herbivorous and are stocked in waters where weed control is required. In the U.S., grass carp are commonly found in golf course ponds and farm ponds, but they have also been introduced into large reservoirs.

Grass carp arrived in the U.S. in 1963 when fish from Taiwan and Malaysia were imported for experiments in weed control. Triploid fish, those with three chromosomes instead of two, were commonly stocked, since they are not capable of reproducing. At least that's the theory. Since grass carp also need a set of very special circumstances in order to spawn successfully, officials reasoned that populations of grass carp could be contained.

The jury is still out in terms of the truth of this. There are reports of spawning grass carp in the Mississippi River and in the Trinity River in Texas, but just because a fish can spawn, it does not necessarily follow that its eggs are fertile or that its offspring will survive in sufficient numbers to create a self-sustaining population.

Family Tree

The grass carp is the sole member of its genus. There are no subspecies. Grass carp are more properly called white amur. The name comes from the Amur River in Russia where grass carp are native. They do not appear to hybridize with other carp in the wild, but in the laboratory grass carp have been successfully hybridized with other carp, notably goldfish and common carp.

Range

In the U.S., the grass carp does not have a range in the sense that we usually use the word. In theory, at least, there are no self-sustaining populations. All of the grass carp you find will have been deliberately placed there to control weeds, will eat weeds until they die, and will be replaced by new grass carp. At least, that's the theory.

Apparently, some folks aren't buying it, because many states forbid the importation of grass carp. If you want to catch a grass carp, you may want to call your state fisheries agency to determine if they're even permitted in your state. Environmentally, there is nothing that would prevent grass carp from living in all of the lower forty-eight states.

Appearance and Size

The grass carp is a more elegant fish than the common carp. The body is oblong and slimmer without the hunched-shoulder look of common carp. The mouth is classified as terminal/subterminal, meaning that it is carried higher on the head than the common carp's is. The lips are not as fleshy and the barbels are absent. Unlike the common carp, grass carp have no spines on their fins. Like the common carp, grass carp have no teeth in their jaws and make use of pharyngeal teeth to process food.

Grass carp are generally dark brown above, transitioning into lighter shades below. The sides of the fish characteristically have a light, golden sheen. There is no evidence of hybridization with other species in the wild, so the coloration of grass carp is generally uniform from fish to fish.

Depending on environmental circumstances, female grass carp mature at roughly twenty-three to twenty-six inches long and at the age of one to eleven years. Males mature at smaller sizes, twenty to twenty-four inches long, and at an earlier age. In warmer climates, especially in the tropics, grass carp mature earlier and at smaller sizes. It's not known how long grass carp can live, but specimens over twenty years old have been recorded.

The ultimate size grass carp can reach may be the subject of some fish stories. Several Chinese researchers have asserted that grass carp can reach sizes of 130 to 400 pounds. While we would love to believe that is possible, no one else has recorded numbers even close to these. The largest grass carp are probably in the fifty- to sixty-pound range for intensively fed, farm-raised fish. In the wild, a twenty- to thirty-pound grass carp is a fine fish, and there may be an occasional forty- to fifty-pound monster waiting to be caught.

Habitat

Adult grass carp prefer densely vegetated areas. Shallow areas are favored, but some researchers report movement to deeper water during winter. In their native waters, adults move to flowing water in the spring of the year when rivers are high and swim upstream to spawning grounds.

The fact of the matter is that you may never meet a grass carp that behaves as it does in the species' native waters. Every grass carp you meet—theoretically—will have been placed in a pond or lake requiring weed control and will not be able to migrate. The recent discoveries of grass carp in rivers suggests that we may have to write a more detailed description of grass carp habitat in a later edition.

Senses

All carp have excellent sensory capabilities, and we believe that all of the senses of grass carp—hearing, smell, taste, and vision—are at least as good as those of the common carp. Although not as much research is available to substantiate this belief, your own experiences flyfishing for grass carp will likely be proof enough. Grass carp are at least as hard to please and as easy to spook as common carp.

Reproduction and Spawning

In theory, the grass carp needs flowing water to be able to spawn successfully. In fact, some research has indicated that if grass carp do not swim upstream for a substantial distance, they can't spawn. Researchers report that grass carp whose upstream journey was limited to one to two miles did not spawn. Additional research indicates that if the eggs can't float downstream, they don't hatch. Some researchers assert that a drift of at least thirty miles is required if the eggs are to hatch successfully.

All this points toward the likelihood that grass carp can't create a self-sustaining population in the habitat U.S. anglers will find them. But if there's one thing the common carp should have taught us, it is that all carp are very tough and very adaptable. Over the long haul, given a choice of betting on the scientists or betting on the grass carp's ability to survive, we're afraid we'd have to bet on the carp.

Grass carp are spring spawners, and if they were to reproduce successfully in the U.S., they would probably spawn in March and April in the southern states and as late as July or August in the north. As is the case with common carp, spawning is a splashy affair. The females are followed by two or more males and spawning takes place near the surface, usually in the center of the river channel. Mating grass carp roll, rub bodies together, and often leap from the water. Finally, a male prods the female's belly with his head to induce delivery of eggs. A ten-pound fish may lay 500,000 eggs, a twenty-two-pound fish over a million. Grass carp eggs hatch about a day after fertilization.

Given the right conditions, grass carp can grow with appalling speed. Growth rates of over two pounds in the first year of life and up to six-and-a-half pounds per year thereafter are not unusual.

Diet

Larval grass carp begin feeding on algae and zooplankton. By the time the fish have grown to three-quarters of an inch, insect larvae, especially that of midges, become an important part of the diet. When a young grass carp achieves an inch in size, its diet switches primarily to plants. However, a grass carp eats animal food throughout its life—especially when plant food items are scarce.

Shoaling and Social Behavior

We believe that the shoaling and social behavior of the grass carp is at least as sophisticated at that of the common carp. When fishing for grass carp, we are as cautious with our wading and as careful with our fly presentation as we are with common carp.

With this general background in hand, it's time to zero-in on some of the specific skills you'll need to become a successful flyfisher for carp. The next thing you'll need to know is how to locate carp and identify their feeding behavior, and that's the subject of the next chapter.

THREE

LOCATING FEEDING CARP

This chapter will help you learn to find carp. Unfortunately, just because you've found carp doesn't mean that you've also found receptive, actively feeding carp. Understanding the difference was one of my earliest and most important lessons.

I arrived at a small lake and gave the water a fast once-over. I noticed a large group of carp milling around just under the surface over some deep water. Closer to shore, I also noticed a few loners rooting around in the shallows. Since I'm as greedy as the next guy, I decided to cast to the group.

Wrong choice! Whatever those milling carp were doing, they weren't feeding. I threw everything at them but my hat, with no success. Finally, I left those fish and moved back to the shallows to take a crack at the loners. A clear behavioral difference was evident. They were moving, stopping occasionally to root in the mud and weeds. These were the feeding fish I was looking for and it didn't take long to hook up. Locating carp and differentiating feeding from non-feeding fish is crucial to successful flyfishing for carp.

Finding Carp

You'll find feeding carp close to food sources. In lakes, carp and many other species of fish find food in fertile bays and sheltered backwaters where abundant plant growth gives cover to insects, crustaceans, mollusks, and baitfish.

Shorelines can offer the same kind of shallow, food-rich environment, so they sometimes attract carp, as do points and shallow, mid-lake structure. Flooded terrestrial vegetation permits carp to forage amid shoreline plants during periods of high water.

Like other fish, carp take advantage of channels, which offer the protection of deep water and access to shallow-water food along the edges of the channels and in the bays or flats to which the channels may lead. Because channels offer both cover and a route along which carp may travel, they can be the first place carp will run when they spook. A quiet excursion along these "highways" in search of moving carp is often a good idea.

When anglers think of feeding carp, they may only picture carp rooting in the mud—they certainly do feed in soft bottoms. Such mucky areas are preferred forage areas, but carp also feed successfully in rocky bays, along areas of rip-rap, and even over gravel, where they vacuum up insects and other small food items.

Before you throw up your hands in disgust because it's apparent that carp can be virtually anywhere in a lake, here are some tips that will help you out.

First, the most likely place to find feeding carp is in weedy, shallow water. In the spring, carp move to the shallows in preparation for spawning. Dark-bottomed bays will warm first, and they deserve your first look. At all times of the year, carp seek food in these same shallow bays and flats that offer both plant life and animal life. Bays with access to deeper water or other cover are preferred, as are areas with soft bottoms, which permit carp to root for insects.

The next place you should check is along shorelines that offer the same kind of food availability. Look for substantial shallow areas along the shore that support plant growth and provide access to cover.

At all times, carp are opportunistic. Massive insect emergences or spinner falls will attract carp no matter what the depth of the water or the nature of the bottom. Because they're omnivorous, carp are equally quick to take advantage of plant seeds on the surface or flooded terrestrial vegetation. If carp are feeding on the surface, it won't be difficult to find them. If you can't see them, you'll probably hear them.

The search for feeding carp will become less frustrating the more you do it, because carp are predictable. If you spot carp rooting in a patch of aquatic weeds one day, you'll probably find them there again the next time you're out. When you do find feeding carp, remember that they are highly mobile. Be prepared to follow them.

As a final tip, let's eliminate a large area of the lake from consideration when searching for feeding carp. Brad and I think it's pretty futile to fish for carp in really deep water. As far as we're concerned, part of the thrill of flyfishing for carp is the opportunity to sight-fish in shallow water and stalk carp. Stealthy wading, crouching, trying to determine which fish to cast to without spooking the rest of the shoal is, in our opinion, the most fun you can have in freshwater.

We spend the majority of our time in water that's shallow enough to wade in, rarely casting into more than ten feet of water. As is the case with all rules, there is an exception to this one. The exception occurs when carp feed on the surface in deep water, and we'll discuss this special circumstance later.

Moving Water

As you might expect, the adaptable carp do very well in moving water, too. They can be found in many of the same lies that trout prefer, although they favor slower water. Like trout, they seek holding areas to obtain shelter from the current, while they frequent other areas for feeding.

The good news is that if you spot a carp in moving water where you'd expect to find trout feeding (such as a riffle), the odds are that the carp is feeding. Carp don't fight the current without a purpose. The bad news is that you may discover to your chagrin that a carp can be tougher to fool than a trout! Because they seek to avoid the current and feed as efficiently as possible, carp also frequent pools.

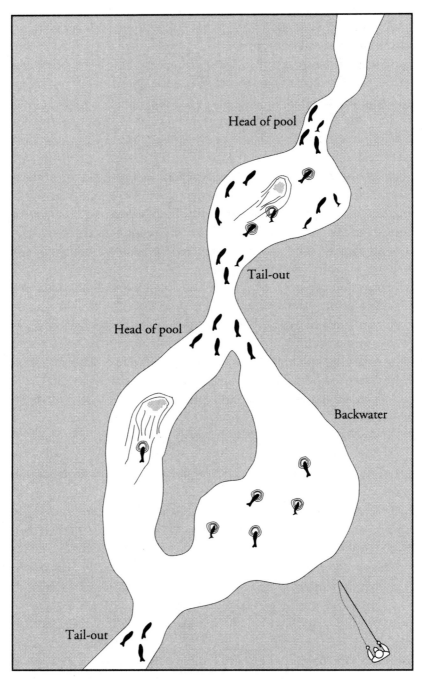

Moving-Water Carp

As you can see from the illustration, a carp in the faster water at the head or tail of a pool is usually a feeding carp. Like trout, they are willing to fight the current in return for the food that faster water funnels to them. They also use whatever cover they can find to gain shelter from the current.

The other carp shown along the edges of the pool and in the eddies and backwaters may be holding or feeding. Because they're not confronted with the need to make a rapid decision, they're likely to be more selective when they do feed.

In many carp streams, backwaters often lack significant current and are overgrown with weeds and algae, making them look like stagnant water. Because there isn't much current, they can also be quite warm. Such factors make these areas very unappealing for a trout, but attractive to carp. These backwaters are worth investigating.

If you're on a trout stream, fishing for carp in a backwater can test your dedication to flyfishing for carp. At this point, some well-meaning fellow will inevitably come along and explain that you're fishing water that holds trout, but you're fishing in a slow backwater that trout avoid. Faced with this situation, you can:

1. Politely thank the man and wait for him to go away. Instead he'll probably insist on doing you a favor by leading you to some "good water."

2. Politely thank the man and keep on fishing. He'll eventually leave, utterly convinced that he's wasted time trying to teach the basics of flyfishing to a moron.

3. Admit that you're flyfishing for carp. You'll discover what sort of angler you've met right away. Some will laugh, some will stare, and some will refuse to believe you. And once in a great while, you'll meet someone who will be eager to learn more about what you're doing.

Water Clarity

Because of their adaptability, you will probably have equal opportunities to find carp in both clear and cloudy water. Some

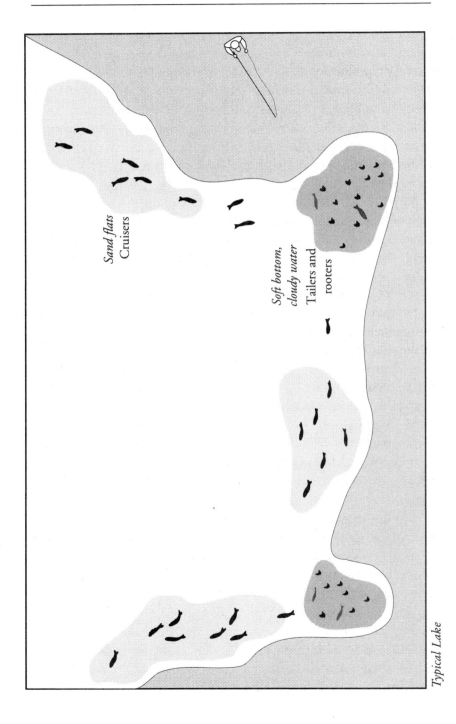

Sand flats
Cruisers

Soft bottom,
cloudy water
Tailers and
rooters

Typical Lake

of our favorite carp lakes offer both. Brad and I routinely fish one lake, illustrated here, where understanding the nature of the bottom is quite important.

You'll find that mucky bays offer more fish, but no sight-fishing. You will have the opportunity to sight-fish, casting to large shoals of carp, when they move from one bay to another through connecting channels, as indicated in the illustration. Watch these areas. Sometimes the carp slow down and forage briefly as they move through.

As you might expect, clear-water and cloudy-water conditions each offer advantages and challenges to the angler. Clear water, for instance, offers the best chance to spot individual fish; on the other hand, the cloudy, muddy water created by feeding carp (we call these "muds") is easy to spot and may lead you to great fishing.

While you have the best chance to see feeding carp in clear water, they are also more likely to spot you, making the approach more challenging. On the practical side, wading is more difficult in the mucky areas where you'll encounter cloudy water.

In clear water, the fish can see the fly and are often more willing to chase it. In cloudy water, the need for accurate casting is increased but fish may not be as finicky or selective. Finally, sight-fishing to individual fish is by far the most fun, but one panic-stricken fish can alarm an entire group in clear water. By fishing into muds and attempting to catch fish from the perimeter, you stand a greater chance of taking several fish from a single group.

You'll find good fishing opportunities for carp in both situations, and you may learn to enjoy one more than the other. Overall, Brad and I think most flyfishers will do better in clear water, where carp can see their flies and they can see the carp. This kind of fishing is the most fun for many people.

But we think a flyfisher shouldn't pass up a good mud with feeding carp in it. Cloudy waters are more difficult to fish because we've all learned to depend on fish seeing our flies. A patient flyfisher with sufficient self-confidence to make repeated casts into muds can be very successful.

Weather and Seasonal Changes

As we've already seen, carp can withstand wide temperature ranges and are tolerant of low oxygen levels and turbidity. These traits make them less sensitive to weather and seasonal changes than most other fish, but a good carp angler will still keep the weather and the season in mind.

When a storm moves through, the downwind side of a lake experiences heavy wave action. Crashing waves stir up the bottom and sweep onshore, pulling plants and terrestrial insects into the water as the waves retreat. The rain that accompanies the storm swells streams and flushes additional food into the lake. This provides exceptionally rich feeding opportunities for carp, and anglers willing to fish blindly into the muddy water or cast at swirls and eddies made by feeding carp will be rewarded.

As is true for other fish, storms or unsettled weather will often put carp off their feed for a few days, but they can be good news for the savvy carp angler who is willing to work during or just after a storm. Overall, consistency in the weather makes for the best carp fishing, just as it makes for the best fishing for any species.

As for seasonal changes, the carp's ability to withstand wide temperature ranges might appear to make the seasons of minor importance, but this is not strictly true. The feeding patterns of carp follow the seasonal cycle of aquatic plants.

In the spring, the shallowest water warms first, plants begin to grow there first, and small fish and insects find food and cover there first. It's in this very shallow water that carp will be found early in the season. They feed there on emerging vegetation and the year's new crop of insects and fry; and they spawn there, where their eggs attach to emerging plants and their young can find food.

As summer approaches, the waters continue to warm and the sun's rays penetrate deeper into the water, permitting plants to grow at greater depths. In shallow ponds, carp can forage efficiently anywhere in the impoundment since plants will be present everywhere. In lakes, carp are able to move deeper and still feed efficiently.

While aquatic insects emerge throughout the spring and summer, the beginning of fall usually marks a dramatic increase in activity on the part of both aquatic and terrestrial insects. Suddenly, carp may be presented with large emergences or spinner-falls and with bonanzas of terrestrial insects such as flying ants, hoppers, or crickets.

This is also the time when many plants distribute their seeds. Milkweed, dandelion, cottonwood, maple, or mulberry seeds may literally carpet the surface of a lake or pond. At this time of year, carp are more likely to feed on the surface and may be more likely to accept a dry fly. This doesn't make them easy to catch, of course. Surface-feeding carp are spooky whenever you find them.

Understanding Carp

You won't have too much trouble finding carp. They're likely to live where you fish and they forage actively enough for you to spot them. But simply finding carp is not enough—you must learn to identify carp behavior and understand what it means. The carp you'll find fall into five general categories.

1. Carp in the shallows, usually in loose shoals.
2. Scattered surface feeders, usually in loose shoals.
3. Carp sunning on the surface in loose shoals or alone.
4. Stationary carp below the surface, often in large shoals.
5. Cruising carp, usually in large shoals.

1. Carp in the Shallows

As you become a carp-flyfishing fanatic, you'll dream of a loose group of carp working their way across a shallow flat. At its most frantic, you'll see tails, fins, and a spreading stain of mud as the carp systematically work their way across the bottom. When this behavior is more restrained, you'll see carp moving slowly across the shallows and individual fish dipping from time to time to snare a bug or piece of vegetation. When the carp are working in a little deeper water, you may see "nervous water" that will remind you irresistibly of bonefish on a tidal flat.

Frantic or restrained, these are actively feeding fish. Look for them, cherish them when you find them, and remember when and where they are feeding. Chances are you'll find them there another day.

For Brad and I, the sight of tailing carp has become the Holy Grail of our carping adventures. Now, I count Brad as a good friend, and I have every reason to believe that he feels the same way about me. But there are limits ...

Brad and I were fishing a ten-acre pond, casting assorted flies at some spring smallmouth that were full of vim and vigor and completely lacking in common sense. I happened to scan the surface of the lake and at the far end, in a little bay, I saw nervous water. Then I saw some tails. And they were *big* tails.

I was faced with an ethical dilemma. Should I tell Brad about the carp and run the risk that two anglers, fishing in a confined area, might put the fish down? Or should I keep my trap shut and quietly work my way over to the fish? As I said, there are limits to friendship. And there was no point to trying to crowd two anglers into that little bay. I decided that it would be best if I fished it alone.

"Well," I said casually, "I guess I'll work my way up along the far side of the lake—maybe pick up a little northern."

"Yeah," said Brad, equally casually, "S'pose I'll move along the other side, after I go water the daisies."

I moved up the bank fifty feet or so until I saw Brad head off into the bushes. Then I hopped out of the water and bush-whacked my way through thick brush and deadfall until I spotted the bay through the brush. The tails were still there!

Crouching, moving as stealthily as I could and planning my first cast carefully, I prepared to enter the water. Just then there was a soft, sighing sound and a fly plopped into my target area. Amazed, I looked across the small bay to see a grinning, crouching Brad.

It's terrible when you discover that you can't even trust your friends.

It's terrible when you discover you can't even trust your friends. (Barry Reynolds)

2. Scattered Surface Feeders

Suddenly, the surface of the water will be broken by gaping mouths, usually proceeding in roughly the same direction. Sometimes they're gulping down insects. At other times they're eating seeds. But at any time, the sight of a group of surface-feeding carp will trigger a mad but quiet scramble to remove a nymph and attach a midge imitation, a hopper, an adult damselfly, or a cottonwood-seed imitation to your tippet.

It's a mad scramble because these fish are usually moving at a fair clip and because they'll suddenly move off at right angles to their course or submerge and surface again just beyond casting range.

The scramble is quiet because these are the spookiest carp that we know of. A stumble as you wade, a splash from your belly boat, a thump as you pole or paddle your canoe or boat, or a too-rapid, careless cast will put them down in an instant. Should this happen, do not despair. Wait and watch. Often, the fish have just ducked under the surface for a moment and will resurface quickly. At other times, they move out of the vicinity. When that happens, they often remain just below the surface and a trail of nervous water or the occasional display of a fin help you stalk them—much more quietly this time.

Incidentally, in England, where carp are revered as a game fish and particularly large carp are caught repeatedly and given names (affectionate and otherwise) by anglers, surface-feeding carp are known as "cloopers," and a carp that is surface feeding is referred to as a "clooping" carp. We think this is a wonderfully appropriate term, for if you're ever close to surface-feeding carp, you'll hear distinct "cloop" sounds as they work their way across the

---

Scattered Surface Feeders

- *Cast to "A" only if you can reposition yourself to avoid spooking the rest of the fish.*
- *Casting to "B" is acceptable, but you're probably better off waiting to cast to "C" or "D."*
- *Your best option is "C." You can sneak this fellow out without alarming other fish.*
- *Another acceptable option is "D," but I'd recommend waiting for the shoal to move ahead slightly to avoid the possibility of lining "C."*

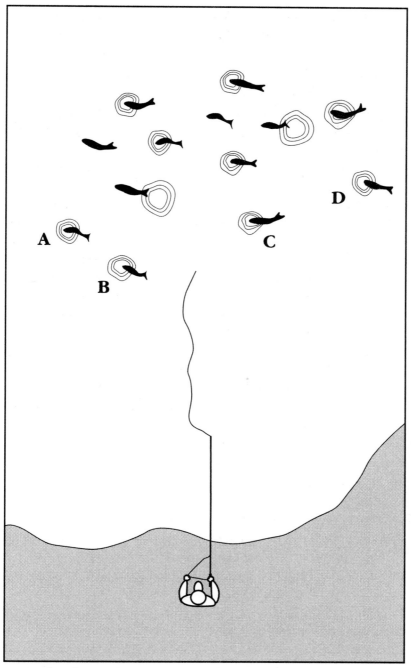

Scattered Surface Feeders

surface of the water, sucking up damselflies, mayflies, midges, and floating seeds.

Brad and I love casting to cloopers. Brad, who casts the way Annie Oakley used to shoot, is especially good at picking trailing cloopers out of the group without frightening off the rest. This is a skill that develops with practice, and it involves waiting until you're certain that you've defined the boundaries of the shoal and are casting to trailing fish, in particular the one closest to you. The illustration may be helpful.

As you can see from the illustration, the angler casts only to fish that can be reached without lining other fish. In the event of a strike, there's a chance (though a small one) of landing a perimeter fish without spooking the rest of the group.

There is yet another option for casting to clooping fish that we present somewhat cautiously. The angler may be able to relocate and pick off a lead fish (as in "A" above) or trail the shoal and cast repeatedly to trailing and perimeter fish (as in "D" above).

This can be great fun if the fish are moving in a uniform direction, but the movements of clooping carp are almost always erratic. In the course of attempting to place yourself where you think they're going to be, you may put the fish down. This process can resemble a rather absurd ballet, with the angler playing the role of the suitor and the carp the role of shy maidens. Like many ballets, it can go on for a very long time. But I urge you to practice The Dance of the Carp; position is the key to success in flyfishing for cloopers.

Early one afternoon, about the time my watch and my belly told me that it was time for a cold soda and a sandwich back at my car, I suddenly saw perhaps fifty cloopers in the bay I was fishing. As cloopers are prone to do, they just appeared there. I saw no seeds. I saw no large insects. They had to be clooping for midges, I reasoned. I tied on a tiny Griffith's Gnat.

Wading in the sort of crouched position that is guaranteed to make the muscles in your lower back tighten into painful knots, I moved off to my left to pick up a trailing fish.

The cloopers moved to the right.

Making sure I had their direction of travel figured out, I reversed my position and moved off to the right. The cloopers made a right-angle turn and headed out to the mouth of the bay where it was too deep for me to wade and too far for me to cast. Cussing mildly, I stood up, easing my back.

The cloopers reversed course and headed directly toward me. Instantly, I went back into my crouch. The carp must have seen a movement, because in a flash they were gone.

I stood up.

The carp reappeared.

I crouched and again moved to cast to a tailer.

The carp reversed course.

The carp and I repeated variations on this theme for the next three hours. I don't know who had more fun that afternoon, me or the carp. I made precisely four casts. I caught exactly one carp. And I had more fun than I've ever had on a bonefish flat.

3. Sunning Carp

You'll run across two kinds of sunbathing carp. Most commonly, you'll be fishing a bay or flat and suddenly a carp, usually alone, will betray its location with the movement of a fin or the sun will glint off its scales. These carp are typically just beneath the surface. Sometimes you'll be very close to the fish, and often, probably due to one of Murphy's more perverse laws, it will be a big fish.

Brad and I don't expect you to believe for a minute that we wouldn't cast to this fish. Carp are opportunistic, and these fish will take advantage of an easy meal just often enough to keep us casting to them. So, when we see a big sunbathing carp, we cast to it!

Unfortunately, we don't catch these fish very often, and we don't think you will, either. A sunbather typically isn't feeding and, perhaps because the fish is indulging in the equivalent of carp daydreams, it's easy to startle. Rapid flight to deeper water usually ensues, accompanied by splashing and a trail of mud, which means there is a danger in casting to this fish. When it runs for cover, it may startle active feeders nearby.

You'll also find sunbathing carp in open water. Though these are also usually solitary fish, sometimes you'll come across a loose group of sun-worshipers. Like the shallow-water fish, these carp are usually just under the surface of the water, and often they will betray their location with a waving fin or tail. Once again, you'll often find yourself very close to these fish.

Most of the time, these fish are just sunning and, when presented with a fly, they will quietly head for the depths. But at other times, they're filter-feeding on tiny plants and animals and may be willing to accept a small nymph that happens to drift their way. The only way to find out is to cast a fly to them.

This can be a more demanding process than you might expect. On a trip to Flaming Gorge Reservoir, where sheer rock bluffs overlook the water, I'd sighted some suspended carp that looked as if they might be worth a cast or two. I managed to work my way down a series of thirty-foot rock walls. Had I known how many casts it was going to take, I might not have chosen to go mountaineering.

Though the carp were moving slowly, they were moving, and my unweighted Woolly Bugger wasn't getting to the fish quickly enough. Thinking I knew the solution to the problem, I added some split shot to my leader. Again, my offering was ignored. It wasn't until I moved to smaller shot, slowing the descent rate to something the carp found appealing on that particular day and at that particular time, that I managed to start catching fish.

As with shallow-water sunbathers, we hook up with these open-water sunbathers just often enough to keep us casting to them. The difference is that when these fish move away from you, they generally do so calmly, so you usually don't have to worry about frightening other fish.

4. Stationary Carp

Stationary, submerged carp are probably the most frustrating quarry of all. These carp are usually found near cover, often in the midst of weed beds, and they are either stationary or moving very

We suggest that he really did catch the fish of a lifetime. (Barry Reynolds)

Tailers are carp that are feeding along the bottom in a head-down position. (Barry Reynolds)

Look for a commotion in the shallows where carp might be rooting around.
(Barry Reynolds)

Grass carp can be regularly persuaded to take a variety of insect imitations.
(Barry Reynolds)

The odds of catching carp on dry flies improve dramatically when carp are consistently feeding on the surface. (Brad Befus)

Shorelines can offer a food-rich environment. (Brad Befus)

We include grass carp because they provide fabulous sport. (Barry Reynolds)

Lighter rods provide great entertainment if you're able to fish where there's not much brush or snags. (Barry Reynolds)

Any carp is strong, and big carp (over fifteen pounds) are really strong. (Bill Rivett)

Have you ever flyfished for carp? (Barry Reynolds)

FAVORITE CARP FLIES

Clouser Swimming Nymph (John Berryman)

Bead-Head Prince Nymph (John Berryman)

Rubber-Legged Hare's Ear Nymph (John Berryman)

Befus' Wiggle Bug
(John Berryman)

Dandelion or Thistle Seed
(John Berryman)

CDC Cottonwood Seed
(John Berryman)

Whitlock Hopper
(John Berryman)

Barr 'Bou Face
(John Berryman)

Reynolds' 'Poxy 'Dad
(John Berryman)

slowly. Because they're so still, you're most likely to notice them only if you're looking very carefully or if a bit of motion from one of these fish catches your eye.

There are two problems with respect to fishing for these carp. One is a tactical problem and the other is a behavioral problem. Tactically, you'll probably find it quite difficult to present these fish with a fly. They are likely to be holding very tight to heavy weed cover, and weaseling a fly to them may be difficult, if not impossible. After snagging a few flies and tearing up some weeds, you're likely to spook these fish, once again startling nearby feeders.

Figuring out the behavior of stationary, submerged carp is, if anything, more difficult than the tactical problems you face. If you can find these fish and figure out a way to cast to them, you must then determine what they are doing. Many times they're lethargic and not feeding, and they will ignore your fly. At other times, these fish have found an especially rich food area and aren't moving because they're literally surrounded by food. These fish will accept a fly.

When confronted with one of these carp, Brad and I make a judgment call. If we think we can drop a fly to the fish without snagging on weeds or startling it, we do so. If it looks like we'll startle the fish and thereby spook other more accessible, more active carp, we'll give the fish a pass. This can result in some very quiet, but very intense negotiations between anglers.

Once Brad and I spotted a group of tailers that were systematically working their way along the shoreline of a bay. Positioning ourselves so that we'd each have a shot at the shoal, we quietly entered the water. Suddenly, Brad froze.

I hissed at him, and he pointed. Although I couldn't see the fish, I knew what he was pointing to. It had to be one or more big, stationary carp. I saw him remove his fly from the keeper. I hissed again and pointed to the tailers that were approaching us. We knew they were feeding and we shouldn't risk putting them down, I reasoned.

Brad shook his head and pointed again. Clearly, he was of the bird-in-the-hand school of thought: the carp you can see and cast

We spotted tailers systematically working their way along the shoreline. (Robert Sweet)

to is better than the carp that might decide to change direction before it gets to you.

I shook my head and pointed at the tailers. He shook his head and stripped some line off his reel. I gave some thought to putting a size 6 Dave's Hopper in his right earlobe.

In the midst of our pantomime, we were interrupted by a loud and cheerful voice from the bank.

"Doin' any good?" yelled the new arrival.

We nearly jumped out of our skins.

"All I ever seen in here is carp," the man shouted.

Brad and I turned our eyes back to the water.

"Not any more," Brad called back sadly.

5. Cruising Carp

Cruisers come in two varieties and you'll need to observe cruising carp carefully to determine which is which.

Although fish aren't known for displaying much in the way of reasoning, the first type of cruising carp will appear to be "purposeful." They travel in a group, usually fairly tightly clustered and heading steadily in one direction.

Casting to these purposeful cruisers is usually a lost cause, for two reasons. First, these fish really are going somewhere and rarely do they stop to investigate a fly. Second, they are usually traveling quickly, and your chances of being able to spot them, cast to them, and have time for your fly to sink to their depth are slim.

The second kind of cruising carp are also unlikely to accept your fly. You'll see a group of carp swimming past, and after a cast or two, they swim out of sight and you're likely to forget about them. Then, anywhere from five to thirty minutes later, you'll spot another group of cruising carp going the same direction. You'll probably cast to them with a similar lack of success. After this happens a couple more times, you'll begin to think you're on a carp highway.

What's happening? What you're seeing is a group of "circulators." As you can see from the illustration, they are roaming in open water in a roughly circular pattern. Periodically, they swim past you. Like the purposeful cruisers, these fish aren't actively feeding.

There may be active feeders among them, however. Those carp, usually traveling in smaller, looser groups, may leave the main group to forage in shallow water. Typically, they'll feed for a time and then rejoin the group of circulators.

Therefore, when carp appear at regular intervals, it's good news! Something is keeping them nearby and often that is food. It's time to begin looking around for small groups of active feeders in the shallows. Do not despair if you don't find them right away. Scan the water, be observant, be patient. These fish slip in and out of the shallows to feed, and just because you don't spot them immediately doesn't mean that you won't spot them a few minutes later.

If you simply can't find any feeding carp, it may be that something has alarmed them and is keeping them out of the shallows. Unfortunately, the thing that has alarmed them may be you, particularly if you've been casting to other game fish. Hungry carp may be waiting for you to go away. Stop fishing for a time or get

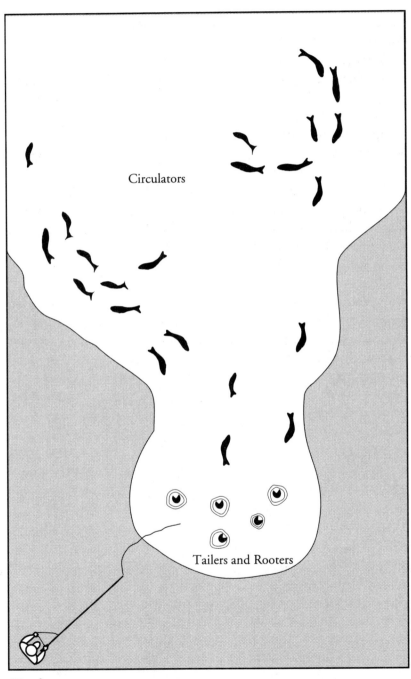

Circulators

Tailers and Rooters

Circulators

out of the water to see if this allows some active feeders to leave the group of circulators.

This process can be maddening. Brad and I were fishing for trout when we happened to see carp swimming by every twenty minutes or so. As far as we were concerned, these were fish that wanted to feed but had been frightened by our repeated casts to nymphing trout. After an exchange of some cryptic hand signals, we left the water as quietly as we could and waited for the carp to relax.

That time the carp didn't relax. They left, moving off suddenly and purposefully into deeper water. What startled them? What was out there that was more appealing to them than the smorgasbord in the shallows? Who knows ... that's carping!

Now you have the tools to locate carp and, by exercising your powers of observation, to recognize whether the carp you've found are feeding or not. With this information in hand, it's time to take a look at what sorts of food carp prefer.

FOUR

WHAT
CARP EAT

I f brevity were our sole concern, this would be the shortest chapter in the book. This is because the most succinct way to describe what carp eat is to say that carp eat virtually anything they can.

Yes, it is true that a carp eats some rather improbable, even nasty items, using both smell and sight to find them. But like other fish, carp focus on the food that is most plentiful and easiest for them to capture, including aquatic insects, crustaceans and mollusks, worms, leeches, larval amphibians, baitfish, and terrestrial insects. In essence, they eat the same sorts of things that other fish eat, and that means we can catch carp on the fly.

In addition, carp eat plant food items, including aquatic plants, seeds that fall in the water, and even terrestrial plants when water is high. Just as in flyfishing for trout, adaptability is the key for the carp angler. This is why, among other things, we've created flies to match the seeds carp slurp from the surface.

Brad and I like to fish a little bay in a local reservoir where a small stream enters. In the mornings, carp often stage at the inlet, picking up nymphs that wash into the bay after a rain. Nymph fishing is very productive. Later in the day when the water warms, insects in the bay begin to come off and we'll find ourselves fishing the bay proper with dries. By late afternoon, when breezes have blown cottonwood seeds into the water, we'll fish seed imitations. By being adaptable, we often take fish all day long.

The issue of what carp eat is complex. What they eat is a function of what is most available to them, and that varies depending on the time of the year, the time of day, the character of the bottom, and other factors. So before we go any further, referral to the following charts and accompanying discussions may be helpful.

Aquatic Insects

All of the classic trout bugs are preyed upon by carp. These include true flies, mayflies, dragonflies, damselflies, caddisflies, and aquatic beetles. Although you'll probably do most of your carp fishing in stillwater, you should know that stream-dwelling carp prey on stoneflies as eagerly as any trout.

Day-in and day-out, Brad and I fish nymphs more than any other type of fly. They're very productive, but that's only part of the story. Nymphs are the most suitable fly for our favorite kind of carp flyfishing, sight-fishing to individual, tailing carp. We've said it before and we'll say it again—this is so much like bonefishing you'll find yourself scanning the surface of the water for sharks.

The following chart provides some general guidance on aquatic life that is available to carp throughout the year.

Organism	Availability/Habitat
Midges	Larvae available year-round in most waters. Adults available in spring, summer, and fall.
Damselflies and dragonflies	Nymphs available all year. Adults available late spring through summer. Shallow, weedy areas preferred.
Aquatic beetles, water bugs	Larvae available all year. Soft-bottomed weedy areas preferred.
Aquatic worms	Found throughout the year. Increases in water flow can make them more available. Found mostly in soft, muddy areas.

Organism *(continued)*	Availability/Habitat
Leeches	Found throughout the year in most waters.
Mayflies	Nymphs available year-round in virtually any water. Depending on species, adults available spring through fall.
Caddisflies	Nymphs available year-round in most waters. Adults available late spring through summer.
Scuds, sowbugs, cressbugs	Available throughout the year. Weedy and rocky areas preferred.

There is a tremendous variation in the sizes of aquatic insects. A midge nymph may be less than one-eighth-inch long, while a large leech may be five inches long. But because the availability of even small insects can be very high at times, carp can feed efficiently on them.

Many years ago, I was present at a Colorado lake during an immense emergence of small mayflies. The surface of the lake was covered with emerging duns. With trembling hands, I tied on a small, gray emerger pattern and made my way to a bay where I could see a commotion caused by feeding fish.

What disappointment! The feeding fish were carp that were moving across the surface like swimming vacuum cleaners, systematically sweeping up both the emergers and any duns that were a bit slow in leaving the water. Disgusted, I watched the fish for a while and then left to find "better" fish.

Today, I'm still disgusted—at myself. I lost what could have been a wonderful day on the water, and I lost it because of a set of preconceptions about carp that I'd accepted blindly.

Crustaceans and Other Food

Carp are known to eat crayfish, clams, mussels, snails, and baitfish. This is a rather mixed-up collection of carp food, but there isn't much that needs to be said about the life cycles of these animals. Hatchling crayfish look like their parents, as do young freshwater mollusks. Within a short period of time, larval fish look like small versions of the adults. Still we want to make a few observations about the most important food items here.

One of the favorite foods of the carp is crayfish. Carp concentrate on smaller crayfish (from one to two inches in size) except when crayfish are molting. If they can find the secretive soft-shelled, molting crayfish, carp will happily gobble up even very large ones.

This size limit also holds true for mollusks. While the pharyngeal teeth of carp crunch small snails, clams, and mussels, there are limits. When we fish snail imitations, rarely do we fish patterns much larger than a pea. We find them to be most effective over soft, weedy bottoms in the spring and fall.

Carp also feed on small fish, but a carp isn't a northern pike! By the time young fish get to be about two inches long, they're usually fast, agile, and savvy enough to avoid cruising carp. When we use small baitfish imitations, we fish them in the spring, at the time baitfish and young-of-the-year are present in large numbers and are at their smallest, weakest, and slowest. Though we've caught carp on baitfish imitations, these patterns aren't as productive on a day-to-day basis as insect imitations.

Organism	Availability/Habitat
Crayfish	Available year-round. Most important early spring to summer (during soft-shell stage). Small crayfish will be eaten at any time. Rocky and weedy areas preferred.
Freshwater mollusks	Clams, mussels, and snails are available year-round. Best in fall when other food begins to die off. Smaller sizes preferred.
Baitfish	Available all year. Early spring best for small, vulnerable baitfish. Shallow waters around perimeter of lakes and streams preferred.

Recently, Brad and I visited a local private farm pond to cast to the large carp there. The ice had come off the pond just a few weeks before, and we thought that hungry carp would be foraging in the shallows. We found the carp, but hook-ups were tough. Finally, Brad nailed a ten-pounder. A few minutes later, he caught another.

Frantically, I cast my nymph in front of the large carp I could see swimming around in the shallows, but I met with no success. After entirely too much casting and far too little catching, I took a break and looked at the fish. They weren't tailing. They weren't clooping. No trails of mud accompanied their steady progress around the shallows. From time to time, individual carp, pairs, or even trios were making fast, purposeful passes through very shallow water. Finally, I caught on.

Those carp could have been stripers. They were smashing into schools of fry, slurping them down as the carp swam through the dense clouds of tiny fish. After a pass through the school, they would withdraw and permit the school to reform. A very small, nearly transparent Clouser Minnow was the answer.

Finally, Brad nailed a ten-pounder, then another one. Those carp could have been stripers. (Barry Reynolds)

Terrestrial Insects

Terrestrial insects become available to carp as a consequence of misadventure. They are blown, fall, or blunder into the water. Both young and adult terrestrials can end up in the drink and carp will feed happily on either. In general, they're most available to carp during and after strong winds or after heavy rains flush them into the water.

Carp have two additional opportunities to consume terrestrial insects. First, in areas where trees and brush extend over the surface of the water, carp may have unusually good opportunities to feed on caterpillars, beetles, and other terrestrials that may fall off or be blown off the brush. Secondly, during periods of high water, carp forage in flooded vegetation, dining on the terrestrials they find there.

When we fish terrestrials, we use hoppers and crickets more than any other flies in this category. They're big, so both angler and fish can see them. They float well and, at certain times of the year, the naturals end up on the water in substantial numbers. Hoppers seem to be a preferred food item for many fish, including carp. We urge you to have hopper imitations on hand.

Organism	Availability/Habitat
Hoppers and crickets	Early summer through fall. Carp have access to hoppers and crickets when they're blown into the water from nearby grassy areas.
Ants	Early summer through fall. Ants also end up in the water during the warm months.
Beetles and larvae	Early summer through fall. Beetles and larva are available, particularly after heavy rains.
Caterpillars	Early summer through fall. Look for them along the bank under trees and brush.
Terrestrial worms	All year. Availability usually a function of heavy rain.

In lakes, particularly in the summer, fish of all species find shade from the sun, food, and cover from predators under branches and brush that overhang the water. Casting near or under the brush will often result in lots of action.

On a trout fishing expedition one hot summer, Brad and I also found shelter from the sun in the shade of some trees and brush. I sat on the bank, munching on a sandwich, while Brad (who would fish thirty hours a day if there were that many hours in a day) threw Woolly Worms under the brush. I don't think the water where he was casting was even a foot deep. About every third cast, the Woolly Worm would disappear in a dainty swirl, Brad would set the hook, and he'd proceed to reel in a sassy little rainbow. All in all, it was quite pretty to watch.

On one cast, the fly landed, he gave it a twitch, and the fly disappeared in the regulation swirl. He set the hook. The water exploded as a big carp that had fallen for the Woolly Worm ran for deeper water. Brad's four-weight might have stopped the fish eventually, but the 6X tippet he was using just wasn't up to the job. Brad and I had a moment to admire the impressive bend the carp put in his rod before the rod abruptly straightened.

You just never know about carp!

Plant Food Items

Seeds from plants such as cottonwood, thistle, dandelion, cattail, and mulberry are available to carp when they drift into the water. As a general rule, seeds become important to carp when large quantities of them are present on the surface.

You've probably seen lakes that look dusty because of the seeds that have blown onto the surface. Usually, this is what it takes to interest carp in surface feeding for seeds. Because seeds are even more at the mercy of the wind than insects trapped in the surface film, the downwind side of lakes and ponds may offer heavier concentrations of them and may, therefore, be preferred by surface-feeding carp.

Plant	Availability
Cottonwood	Summer through early fall.
Thistle	Late summer through fall.
Dandelion	Mid-spring through fall.
Cattail	Midsummer through fall.
Mulberry	Midsummer through fall.

Carp also dine on aquatic and terrestrial vegetation when it's available to them. They seem to prefer tender young plants, although you may find it difficult to create flies to imitate this greenery!

Several years ago, as I was making my first faltering steps toward becoming carp crazy, I was fishing a local lake. Things were slow, but I did notice some carp cruising just beneath the surface. From time to time they would pluck something out of the film. For lack of anything better to do, I tried a few small dry flies. Zilch.

Reasoning that they were feeding on emergers, I tried that route. Again, no luck. I began to become really curious. Scanning the water, I noticed that there was some mayfly and damselfly activity. The carp should have been eating them, but they weren't. Fixing my attention on one carp, I vowed to keep my eyes on it until I saw it rise. Obligingly, the carp rose and delicately slurped a cottonwood seed from the surface.

My mouth dropped. It never occurred to me that the carp were visiting the salad bar when meatier items were available. I rummaged through my fly box, looking for anything that might resemble a cottonwood seed. Luckily, I found a couple of adult damsels that I'd tied with CDC wings. A bit of minor surgery (amputations, really), and I was in business.

Where To Find What

Carp really do eat just about anything, but there is a way to sort it all out. In the balance of this chapter, we'll approach the issue of what carp eat from the perspective of the areas and circumstances where you're likely to fish for them. While carp can forage in mud and ooze in twenty feet of water, it's unlikely you'll

Best of all, you'll be able to see shallow-water carp and sight-fish to them.
(Robert Sweet)

be trying to catch those fish with fly tackle. Therefore, we'll concentrate on situations in which we think you'll be most likely to
find feeding carp and flyfish for them.

Carp in shallow water, gravel bottom, few weeds

In this situation, tailing and rooting fish are common, and often
the carp move slowly, grubbing systematically for the rich har-
vest of aquatic animals living on the bottom. Gravel and small
pebbles offer lots of nooks and crannies that hide insects and
crustaceans, but carp are strong and literally dig up their prey as
they move across the bottom.

Best of all, you'll be able to see the carp and sight-fish to them.
Although the carp know that they are very visible, they sometimes concentrate on feeding so much that they'll tolerate a bad
presentation or a stumble on the part of the angler.

Vegetation is often sparse over a gravel bottom and carp feeding in these areas are probably in search of meat. Food items
include the following:

• Nymphs, larvae, and pupae. Since the population density of insects is likely to be high, they're the food source that carp are most likely to find as they feed along the bottom. For this reason, we recommend that you have a variety of generic nymphs. Although we don't know exactly why, carp exhibit a clear preference for rust-colored nymphs. They outperform black, gray, and olive offerings pretty consistently. However, there are times when other colors are productive. If you're rust-colored offerings are being ignored, and you're confident of your presentation and sure that the fish are feeding on nymphs, try changing colors.

• Aquatic worms. Worms and leeches are common among small rocks and pebbles. Any of several worm or leech imitations—from tiny bloodworm and tubifax imitations up to medium-sized leech patterns—rate as our second choice when fishing over a pebble bottom.

• Small crayfish. It must be tough to be a crayfish. Everything eats them (including one of the authors of this book). Carp also dine happily on crayfish because their pharyngeal teeth allow them to crush even fairly large ones. We use three-quarter-inch to one-inch crayfish patterns, because it is these smaller crayfish that are more likely to be found in this environment. Bigger crayfish are usually found among larger rocks where they can find shelter. Crawfish patterns are particularly effective in the spring or when they molt their shells.

• Snails and other mollusks. This is a tough one for us. Researchers who have sampled the contents of carp stomachs report that carp feed on snails and small freshwater clams and mussels, which they crush with their pharyngeal teeth. This, by the way, provides one indication of the power of those teeth! However, snails and mollusks aren't exactly noted for possessing the kind of action that a flyfisher uses to attract fish. We've tried a few snail patterns over pebbly bottoms (other mollusks are scarce where we live), but overall they are the least productive patterns. We find that snail patterns work best over soft bottoms in the fall.

Carp in shallow water, sandy bottom, few weeds

A sandy bottom contains little in the way of organic matter that supports plant or animal life, and pickings for carp are slim. In addition, the barren waterscape has little shelter for small organisms. To make matters worse, carp are very exposed and very nervous when they're over a sandy bottom. Next to open-water surface-feeders, these may be the spookiest of all carp.

Often the fish found in this environment are moving from one productive feeding area to another, and any tailing or rooting behavior is either force of habit or a quick stab at one of the few critters living in this freshwater desert. Because these fish are covering the bottom quickly, your fly must sink to depth quickly. Weighted flies are definitely in order. Though carp are not the suckers (no pun intended) for flash and glitter that some other fish are, this is one time when a bit of advertising may be helpful. Often a shiny bead-head will provide both needed weight and just a hint of "come hither" to the carp.

In this situation, we don't really try to imitate anything in particular with the flies we choose. The fish aren't feeding systematically, and it's our feeling that getting the fly in front of the fish and getting its attention are the challenges in this case. Flashy nymphs are our first choice.

Carp in shallow water, rocky bottom, few weeds

These areas can be very productive, especially where rocks and boulders meet gravel or mud bottoms, such as where a rocky dam-face meets the bottom of the lake proper. By our definition, a rocky bottom is one in which the rocks are too big for carp to shove around as they root. Typically, these rocks are the size of tennis balls or larger. Tailing behavior is reasonably common, and as was the case with gravel bottoms, rocky bottoms offer an opportunity to sight-fish for feeding carp. For a variety of reasons, however, this fishing environment is a bit more challenging.

Obviously, wading over this kind of bottom can be exhausting and even dangerous. Though the fish will be visible, they'll be wary. There just aren't as many critters per square foot that the carp can get to by rooting and grubbing, which means that the carp aren't as focused on feeding and are more aware of their surroundings. Lower food density also means that carp are likely to cover the bottom more quickly than is the case over a gravel bottom. The likelihood that your fly will get snagged increases, as does the opportunity for a hooked carp to break your tippet on the rocks.

On the bright side, larger nooks and crannies among the boulders mean that bigger prey items can find shelter. This is the domain of minnows, more sizable crayfish, and the like. Again, good populations of nymphs and smaller crustaceans are very likely to be present, although carp may not be able to turn over a head-sized rock to get at them.

Because food items are larger in this environment, everything we cast to feeding carp is larger. This means two-inch to three-inch crayfish imitations; larger nymphs, such as stoneflies, hellgrammites, and crane fly nymphs; and leech imitations, such as Black Woolly Buggers and Barr 'Bou Faces. Depending on the depth of the water, a bit of weight may be helpful. If you find yourself fishing this sort of terrain often, the addition of weed guards robust enough to permit your fly to be slithered over rocks or a selection of inverted flies may also be a good idea.

Carp in shallow water, soft bottom, scattered weeds

Ah, yes, carp rooting around in the weeds and the mud. This is the picture of carp that most anglers conjure up when the fish are mentioned. There's no question that carp do feed in this fashion, but for the flyfisher, such a scenario requires some special considerations.

You'll find the carp feeding aggressively in shallow water or in flooded terrestrial vegetation. The soft bottom permits extensive rooting and grubbing by the carp, and in this fertile food-factory environment, the food-per-square-foot figures are high. Often, the carp move slowly and systematically in such areas and they may appear to feed on both plant and animal food items. But all may not be as it first appears.

Although carp do eat plants and are often found uprooting plants, many times this activity is simply part of their search for buried or burrowing insects. (The English, who sometimes fish for carp with plant baits, may have some things to teach us in this area.)

As they root in the soft sediments, clouds of mud and disturbed detritus shield the feeding carp, and as a result these fish can be the least wary of all carp. On a couple of occasions, when carp have been feeding in flooded terrestrial vegetation in very shallow water, we've even been able to poke them with a rod tip without obtaining much reaction. Such areas are usually packed with weeds, deadfall, and brush.

In these muddy shallows it's difficult to determine a carp's food choices. At one time or another, virtually everything that lives in freshwater spends some time in these areas, either spawning, feeding, growing, or mating there. The good news is that almost anything you have in your fly box has the potential to work. The bad news is that, just as is the case with humans at a buffet table, at times your quarry may pass up the more mundane items on the menu and concentrate on fancier munchies.

With that in mind, our first choice of fly in this environment tends to be a nymph or worm imitation. We think this is what carp are most likely to find in significant numbers. In particular, midge larvae, damselfly and dragonfly nymphs, and beetle larvae (grubs) have been productive for us. Worm and leech imitations are also very productive.

Next on the fly list are imitations of "crud." When you observe feeding carp, you'll note that often a period of vigorous rooting is followed by a period of eating what they've stirred up. "Crud" flies (a few turns of rabbit or marabou on a small hook) are intended to imitate the stuff the carp have rooted up.

It's a good time to use imitations of the small and the weak. Many rather feeble creatures, such as polliwogs, salamanders, leeches, and very young fry, live in these quiet, warm shallows. In the fall of the year, as vegetation dies off and insects become dormant, we fish snail patterns with success.

There is another option when flyfishing for carp feeding in the shallows: dry flies that imitate adult aquatic and terrestrial insects. Your success depends on knowing when fishing dry flies is really feasible. Adult insects can suddenly become available to carp when a hatch begins. The shallow bays where carp like to feed are preferred habitat for many species of mayflies, caddisflies, damselflies, and dragonflies. Terrestrial insects blunder into the water regularly and sometimes, as is the case with flying ants, in substantial numbers.

We suspect that, like many flyfishers, you prefer to fish with dry flies whenever possible. We sympathize; so do we. But we have one reservation—muddy water makes it tough for the carp to see your fly. Our recommendation is to watch the carp carefully. If they take an occasional fly from the surface or if you see lots of bugs on the water, have at it. The odds of catching carp on dry flies improve dramatically when carp are consistently feeding at the surface.

Carp feeding on the surface

Both of the following statements are true. Casting dry flies to carp feeding on the surface may be the most fun you can have with a fly rod in freshwater. Casting dry flies to carp feeding on the surface will turn you into a barking lunatic.

Sometimes you'll find carp in shallow bays, clooping away at a hatch. Other times, you'll find them in open water, picking seeds from the surface with the efficiency of a vacuum cleaner. At first blush, it's a dream come true. All you need to do is position yourself in their direction of travel, cast the appropriate fly in front of them, and wait for an obliging carp to rise to it. Sometimes it really does work like this.

And sometimes it doesn't. In our experience, carp usually don't begin to surface feed until the water is nearly covered with a food item. In the case of insects, this means a carpet of mayflies or flying ants. In the case of plant-food items, carp begin surface feeding when the water is covered with cottonwood or dandelion tufts to the point where it looks like a light snow has fallen. You can probably appreciate the carp's position. If you could forage in the food-rich bottom without exposing yourself to predators, it would take a heavy supply of food on the surface to persuade you to leave the depths.

While these fish may not be selective in the maddening sense that trout can be, they're likely to exhibit a strong preference for the food that they've become accustomed to during their surface feeding. At best, they will often simply ignore an unfamiliar offering. At worst, a strange thing on the surface may frighten them.

There are a couple of tactical concerns that also need to be mentioned with respect to surface-feeding carp. First, it always pays to determine the characteristics of the insects and plant life of the water you're fishing and to take the time to look at the surface of the water to determine what the fish are eating. For example, one of the lakes we love to fish is Elevenmile Reservoir in Colorado. When this lake has one of its amazing damselfly hatches, carp have a field day feeding on the nymphs and emerging adults. If we're visiting Elevenmile, we have both damselfly adult and nymph imitations at hand. Although we don't know what the "bonanza" insect is in the areas you fish, we're sure that there is one and that carp (and everything else in the water) will take advantage of the feeding opportunities these massive hatches represent.

Second, it's important to remember that, although you're casting dry flies, the carp you're casting to have the potential to be larger and much stronger than the fish you're used to. Making a habit of fishing size 28 midges to fifteen-pound carp is a sure way for an angler to wind up in a twelve-step program of some kind. When carp are clooping for midges, we usually elect to throw a midge pattern, such as a Griffith's Gnat, in at least a size 16. It takes the carp just a tad longer to straighten these larger hooks.

Plant food items are favored by surface-feeding carp. Any of the tufted airborne seeds, such as milkweed, cottonwood, and dandelion, can provoke surface feeding if present in large quantities.

Since the seeds are obvious on the surface of the water, an angler has an excellent opportunity to take advantage of this situation.

In addition, duckweed (tiny green plants that drift just below the surface) or other aquatic vegetation that has been torn up by weather or boat propellers can also attract surface-feeding carp. We've already made reference to "crud flies" and to the fact that English bait anglers use a variety of plant items. Have we tied a weed fly? No, not yet. But we might still think about it, particularly with respect to grass carp.

As we've mentioned, the opportunistic carp also choose meatier food items, including emergers, duns, and spinners—provided that the density of the hatch is reasonably high. Day-in and day-out, carp probably eat more midges than any other surface insect. Heavy mayfly or caddisfly emergences and spinner-falls also bring carp to the surface.

In some parts of the country, flying ant hatches rival mayfly hatches. Hoppers, terrestrial beetles, and caterpillars become available to carp after high winds have blown large numbers of them onto the water. Carp take advantage of these hapless terrestrials if good numbers of them are available. A fellow carp-crazy who fishes for his carp in Colorado's Cache La Poudre River has a favorite carp fly—hoppers, fished dry or drowned.

Cruising carp

Cruising carp are going somewhere. As discussed in Chapter 3, they are not typically feeding and are moving quickly. Many times, you won't even see cruising carp. But when you do, you'll want to cast to them, particularly if you've begun to catch carp in other situations. We cast to them, too, but we try not to get too annoyed when nothing works.

Since these carp usually aren't feeding, the problem is not to present them with something they'll eat, but to present them with something that will persuade them to eat. Compounding the problem is the need to place the fly quickly in front of a rapidly moving fish.

Grass carp surprised us by taking flies that imitate insects. (Barry Reynolds)

In our view, this is another time to try a carp-attractor fly, rather than attempting to mimic a particular food item. This means weight, a somewhat larger fly than usual, and a bit of "here-I-am" in the form of flash, glitter, or bright color.

But most of all, you must understand that these fish are unlikely to stop for your fly. Cast to them, cuss at them if you must, but don't let your lack of success keep you from fishing for carp in other, more productive situations.

A Word About Grass Carp

Grass carp exhibit all of the behavioral patterns that we've described in the book thus far: tailing, clooping, and cruising, for example. Because of their strong preference for plant-food items, they are much more likely to be found in areas of heavy weed growth and less likely to be found foraging over gravel or boulders.

When Brad and I began fishing for grass carp, we weren't surprised to find them where the weeds were thick. We weren't surprised that they were feeding heavily on plants. What did surprise us is what sort of flies they took—they hit flies that imitated bugs.

In fact, the grass carp we've cast to take insect imitations with such regularity that we've never found it necessary to embark on the creation of a "weed fly." The closest we've come to such a fly is the occasional use of brown, green, or olive "crud flies."

As is the case with common carp, the immediate issue is to get the fly in front of a grass carp without spooking it or its fellows. For us, a bigger issue is deciding what is actually going on.

Do grass carp eat more insects than most people think? Or is the grass carp simply responding on reflex to a moving target? We just don't know. All we can say with any authority is that, in addition to "seed flies" and "crud flies," grass carp can be regularly persuaded to take a variety of insect imitations.

A final, thoroughly confusing, note about grass carp is in order. A local suburb holds a fishing derby every year at a nearby lake that supports good populations of bass, trout, and grass carp. Each year, the top three places routinely go to the lucky anglers who manage to catch the large grass carp that frequent the lake. Last year was no exception.

What were these three large grass carp taken on? We're glad you asked.

First place: spinnerbait

Second place: crankbait

Third place: spoon

We are still trying to figure out what kind of aquatic vegetation is imitated by a crankbait.

———

Now that you have an understanding of what sort of things carp like to see on the menu, the next chapter will discuss some of the flies we use to imitate these food items and what sorts of presentations you can use to make your bogus dinner item more appealing than the real thing.

FIVE

CARP FLIES

A s we learned in the previous chapter, carp eat a wide variety of foods. Aquatic and terrestrial insects are eaten regularly. Crustaceans and mollusks are likely to wind up on the carp's dinner table, as are small fish and amphibians. Unlike most fish, carp are also partial to "salad bar" items in the form of seeds and aquatic and terrestrial plants. What this means is that carp are likely to inspect just about anything as a potential food item, even if it comes from your fly box. What this doesn't mean is that carp are easy to fool! On the contrary; we've found carp to be every bit as selective as any sport fish, if not more so.

Because carp dine on so many different kinds of food, carrying a good selection of patterns is important. In fact, we recommend approaching your carp fly selection in the same manner you would your trout fly selection. Match the hatch when you can. Study the waters you fish and make an effort to have imitations of the organisms you find. Carry some of the "seed flies" described in this chapter. While not for everyday use, they can save the day for the carp flyfisher. We also encourage you to try your own favorite flies on carp—particularly if you already fish lakes and know the insects in your area.

Over the past several years, Brad and I have fished for carp in large reservoirs, small ponds, and rivers. Often, we've been relative strangers to the waters we fished. The fly patterns in this chapter are those that have been most successful for us.

We're constantly learning more with each trip we make. Much of what we've learned has come about in the traditional way, through trial and error. Still more information has come from fellow carp fanatics who have generously shared what they've learned. We're certain that there's room for much more experimentation in the world of carp flies.

As a result of our experiences, we found a number of flies and tactics that worked, and many more that didn't. Over the years, we've developed confidence in the flies presented in this chapter and in the tactics we use to fish them. We think they'll work for you, too.

Subsurface Flies

On a day-to-day basis, we think you'll be casting nymphs to carp more than any other type of fly. There are several reasons for this. First, in most waters nymphs are very common and carp can feed on them easily. Second, more so than other fish, carp are designed to feed on nymphs. Their underslung mouths, protractile lips, and powerful rooting and digging abilities make them very efficient nymph-eaters. Finally, because they cast well and sink fast, nymphs give the flyfisher the ability to present a fly to feeding carp with accuracy and at an appropriate depth.

Some of the nymph and other subsurface patterns that follow imitate specific insects, while others are more impressionistic. However, they all have one thing in common—they catch carp.

Clouser Swimming Nymph (John Berryman)

Clouser Swimming Nymph

Hook:	Nymph, 3XL, e.g., Tiemco TMC 200R, sizes 8 and 10
Thread:	Fluorescent orange
Weight:	Lead wire
Tail:	Rusty brown rabbit fur
Abdomen:	Rusty brown rabbit fur, dubbed
Wing case:	Peacock herl
Legs:	Mottled brown hen saddle hackle, palmered
Thorax:	Rusty brown rabbit fur, dubbed

When Brad and I speak of this fly, it is almost with religious fervor. This is THE fly, our #1 producer. It has fooled a lot of carp, and Brad and I almost always make our first casts with this fly. Depending on color, the Clouser Swimming Nymph imitates leeches, damselfly nymphs, dragonfly nymphs, fleeing soft-shell crayfish, or even small baitfish and tadpoles. In addition to the rusty version shown here, consider tying some Clousers in olive, black, and gold. Fish this fly deep. Fish this fly shallow. Fish it slow. Fish it fast. But fish it!

Bead-Head Prince Nymph (John Berryman)

Bead-Head Prince Nymph

Hook:	Wet fly or nymph, 1XL, e.g., Tiemco TMC 3761, sizes 10-16
Head:	Gold bead
Thread:	Black
Tail:	Brown turkey biots
Rib:	Flat gold tinsel
Abdomen:	Peacock herl
Legs:	Brown hackle
Wing:	White turkey biot

When carp are cruising or tailing in the shallows, the Bead-Head Prince is one of our favorite flies. The bead head provides some extra weight to get the fly down to the carp's level quickly. We find the Prince to be a good producer throughout the year. The most productive way to fish this fly is to lead the fish when you cast and allow the fish to come up on the sinking fly. Then, slowly inch the fly away and get ready!

Woolly Bugger (John Berryman)

Woolly Bugger

Hook:	Streamer, 3XL, e.g., Tiemco TMC 9395, sizes 4-10
Thread:	To match body color
Tail:	Black marabou fibers, Flashabou on each side
Hackle:	Black rooster saddle hackle, palmered
Body:	Peacock herl or black chenille
Rib:	Fine copper wire

Brad caught his first carp on a Woolly Bugger, and as he recounts the story, it's easy to see how an otherwise sane angler could suddenly become a carp-crazy.

He was fishing for bass at a lake near his home, blind-fishing the edge of a dense weed bed in a fairly shallow bay. Things had been slow, so when he felt a slight bump during the retrieve, he immediately cast back into the same area and began a slow strip.

In the midst of a strip, the line simply stopped. He set the hook, and the fish began a series of violent head-shakes. With the growing suspicion that he had a world-record bass on, he tried to settle down so that he could land the fish. Half an hour and a lot of perspiration later, he managed to bring the fish up to his float tube. He was amazed to discover that he'd hooked a thirty-six-inch carp! At that moment, his perception of carp changed. By any standards, the fish had fought magnificently. That was thirteen years ago, and over the years, his appreciation for the fish has only grown.

By the way, Brad also ties his Woolly Buggers in an all-white version. They're a favorite snack of grass carp.

Rubber-Legged Hare's Ear Nymph (John Berryman)

Rubber-Legged Hare's Ear Nymph

Hook:	Wet fly or nymph, 1XL, e.g., Tiemco TMC 3761, sizes 10-16
Weight:	.015″ lead wire
Thread:	Black
Tail:	Hare's mask guard hairs
Rib:	Fine oval gold tinsel
Abdomen:	Natural hare's ear, dubbed (also rust, olive, black, ginger, etc.)
Wing Case:	Mottled turkey quill
Thorax:	Hare's ear, dubbed (to match abdomen color)
Legs:	Small white rubber strands

Here's a variation of an old favorite that works well for carp. Everyone knows how effective a Hare's Ear Nymph is for many species of fish. The deadly Hare's Ear is just as effective for carp, and this fly is a must in any serious carp angler's fly box. The addition of rubber legs makes this fly especially appealing to carp, and I like to cast it to carp that behave as though they've seen everything.

Barr's Damselfly Nymph (John Berryman)

Barr's Damselfly Nymph

Hook:	Nymph, 3XL, e.g., Tiemco TMC 200R, sizes 8 and 10
Thread:	Olive
Tail:	Olive marabou fibers
Rib:	4X tippet material
Shellback:	Clear plastic strip from Baggie
Body:	Olive brown rabbit fur, dubbed
Legs:	Olive-dyed grizzly hen hackle
Eyes:	Extra-small mono

There are plenty of damselfly nymph patterns available to the angler, but John Barr's rendition works so well on so many fish species (including carp) that it's our first choice. During a damselfly hatch, carp engage in a feeding frenzy as they gorge on nymphs. Since damselfly nymphs are efficient predators and strong swimmers, fishing this fly with short, quick strips is usually most productive.

Barr's Dragonfly Nymph (John Berryman)

Barr's Dragonfly Nymph

Hook:	Streamer, 6XL, e.g., Tiemco TMC 300, sizes 4-8
Thread:	Olive
Tail:	Black marabou fibers
Ribbing:	3X or 4X tippet
Shellback:	Clear plastic strip from Baggie
Abdomen:	Olive brown Scintilla Dubbing, colored on top with black permanent marker
Legs:	Black hen neck hackle
Thorax:	Olive brown Scintilla Dubbing, colored on top with black permanent marker
Eyes:	Small mono

Dragonfly nymphs can be an extremely important food item for carp. They are found in dense vegetation, around decaying detritus and submerged timber, and over rocky bottoms. We like to cast these flies along the edges of dense weed beds, blind-fishing with short, erratic strips. They are equally deadly when sight-fishing to feeding carp during late spring and early summer.

Bead-Head Stonefly Nymph (John Berryman)

Bead-Head Stonefly Nymph

Hook:	Streamer, 6XL, e.g., Tiemco TMC 300, sizes 8-12
Head:	Gold bead
Thread:	Brown
Tail:	Gold turkey biots
Antennae:	Gold turkey biots
Rib:	Ginger Swannundaze
Abdomen:	Gold Antron
Wing Case:	Brown turkey quill, lacquered
Legs:	Brown hackle

Stonefly nymph imitations produce particularly well in rivers. We've found this fly to be especially effective in the late spring and early summer. Though stoneflies are typically found in moving water, we've had success with these flies in stillwater, as well. The pattern given above is for golden stoneflies. Substitute black materials and thread for a black stonefly imitation.

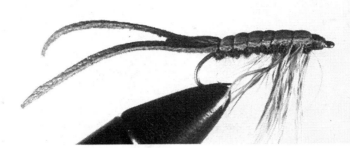

Befus' Wiggle Bug (John Berryman)

Befus' Wiggle Bug

Hook:	Nymph, 3XL, e.g., Tiemco TMC 200R, sizes 8-12
Thread:	Brown
Tail:	Brown Bugskin, trimmed to a V-shape
Shellback:	Brown Bugskin
Body:	Rusty brown rabbit fur, dubbed
Rib:	4X tippet material
Legs:	Mottled brown hen saddle hackle

In time, you will run across carp that have seen one fly too many or nervous carp that are feeding in an exposed position. These fish are smart and spooky. At such times, the Wiggle Bug, weighted or unweighted, may be what you need. Unweighted, these flies land quite softly and sink very slowly. The long tails give the Wiggle Bug a tremendous amount of movement and a lifelike appearance, which often fools the most skeptical carp.

The weighted version of this fly was actually designed first. Brad used to visit a small lake where he watched a spinfisher, who was casting yellow and chartreuse plastic jigs for bass and panfish, commit utter mayhem on carp. The original, weighted Wiggle Bug was developed by Brad to mimic the motion made by soft plastic jigs like the Mr. Twister. We tie Wiggle Bugs in yellow and chartreuse, but carp seem to prefer the more natural look of rust and olive.

Barr's Bead-Head Fup (John Berryman)

Barr's Bead-Head Fup

Hook:	Wet fly or nymph, 1XL, e.g., Tiemco TMC 3761, sizes 8 and 10
Thread:	Black
Head:	Gold bead
Tail:	Olive or black marabou fibers
Rib:	Fine gold wire
Body:	Peacock herl or black Crystal Chenille
Hackle:	Brown or grizzly
Legs:	White rubber strands

Developed by the innovative John Barr, the Fup might be considered to be a sort of "Super Bugger." Fups are great prospecting flies when blind-fishing for carp is necessary. They work equally well when casting to carp in muds, apparently because the white legs and gold bead show up well in discolored water.

Midge Larva (John Berryman)

Midge Larva

Hook:	Nymph, 3XL, e.g., Tiemco TMC 200R sizes 16 and 18
Head:	Peacock herl (option: bead head with peacock herl collar)
Thread:	Red
Body:	Red Larva Lace

The Midge Larva, tied with a bead head when a fast-sinking fly is needed or without for fishing the surface film, is an excellent early spring pattern. Other insect activity is often at a minimum at this time of year. Tied with a bead head, a Midge Larva will also occasionally persuade those maddening, stationary, open-water carp to take a fly. In this case, allowing the fly to sink close (but not too close) to the sulking carp is the key.

San Juan Worm (John Berryman)

San Juan Worm

Hook:	Nymph, 3XL, e.g., Tiemco TMC 200R, sizes 8-16
Thread:	Flat waxed nylon to match body color
Underbody:	Flat waxed nylon to match body color
Body:	Ultra Chenille or Vernille in red, olive, brown, tan, black, or pink

If, as people say, there is virtue in simplicity, then the San Juan Worm is a very virtuous fly. It is certainly a very effective fly. We use this simple tie in both stillwater and rivers, but we find the Worm particularly effective over soft, muddy bottoms in lakes and ponds. Are San Juan Worms taken for aquatic worms? For beetle larvae? All we know is that they are taken!

There seems to be general agreement that red is a particularly effective color, but don't be afraid to fish more natural renderings in olive, black, brown, rust, and "worm-pink." While the specimen we photographed is a rather beefy example of the Worm, we find that very small renditions work well, too. Extremely slow, steady retrieves right on the bottom seem to be the ticket in stillwater, while a nymph-style, dead-drift presentation works well in the current.

Surface Flies

The opportunity to cast dry flies to carp is not a common occurrence. But dries emphatically have their place and casting to cloopers can be among the most enjoyable, challenging, rewarding—and frustrating—aspects of flyfishing for carp.

Where we live in Colorado, mid- to late spring offers some excellent midge fishing, and not just for trout. On one spring day, I made a trip to a local lake. The surface was covered with midges. What I didn't immediately see were the very large carp delicately sipping them from the surface. Once I figured out what was going on, I tied on a size 18 Griffith's Gnat and cast it quietly in the path of a cruising feeder.

As the big fish obligingly clooped my fly from the film, I raised my rod. The water erupted the moment I felt the weight of the fish, and things began to get very exciting. I was fishing with a four-weight rod and a 6X tippet. (I was supposed to be fishing for bluegills.) The thrashing and splashing went on for what seemed a long time, but eventually a thirty-five-inch, twenty-pound carp lay at my feet. Don't ignore dries!

With respect to dries, the question of whether to give them action becomes important, particularly in stillwater. To twitch or not to twitch? Brad and I follow—not very religiously—a very general rule. If surface-feeding carp appear to be relaxed (feeding consistently and moving fairly predictably), we'll consider a twitch. If they're spooky, we won't.

When we do use action, we gear it to the size of the naturals we're imitating. Large or strong naturals (such as adult damselflies, hoppers, and crickets) are more likely to create a visible commotion on the surface, and we'll give more action to these flies. Small or weak naturals are less likely to create a commotion, and we fish these flies with little or no action.

We cheerfully admit that we've muttered curses as we've watched a carp swim right past a fly that it might have taken had we the courage to give the fly a twitch, and that we've also put down more shoals of precious cloopers than we'd care to think about because of a too-vigorous twitch. That's part of carp fishing!

Griffith's Gnat (John Berryman)

Griffith's Gnat

Hook: Dry fly, e.g., Tiemco TMC 100, sizes 14-18
Thread: Olive
Rib: Fine gold wire
Body: Peacock herl
Hackle: Grizzly, palmered

A fine, general-purpose midge imitator. We usually fish this fly without adding any action.

Befus' Parachute Emerger (John Berryman)

Befus' Parachute Emerger

Hook:	Shrimp/caddis pupa, e.g., Tiemco TMC 2487, sizes 16 and 18
Thread:	Gray
Tail:	Rusty brown Antron yarn
Abdomen:	Tannish-brown Scintilla Dubbing
Wing Post:	1/8″ white closed-cell foam
Hackle:	Medium dun
Thorax:	Muskrat fur, dubbed

Brad's Parachute Emerger is one of those wonderful flies that, depending on size and color, can imitate many species of emerging mayflies and midges or even a mating-midge cluster. Brad and I watched a fellow carp angler, casting a size 20 Parachute Emerger on a 6X tippet, hook, battle, and finally land a thirteen-pound clooper. A worthy accomplishment by any angler! We throw this fly to cloopers when we can see no sign of insects or seeds on the surface of the water.

Callibaetis CDC Biot Mayfly (John Berryman)

Callibaetis CDC Biot Mayfly

Hook:	Dry fly, e.g., Tiemco TMC 100, sizes 14 and 16
Thread:	Tan
Underwing:	Brown CDC
Overwing:	Natural wood duck
Tail:	White Betts' tail fibers
Abdomen:	Light tan turkey biot
Thorax:	Tan Superfine Dubbing

This pattern and the one that follows are excellent mayfly imitations. Read the description for the Callibaetis CDC Biot Mayfly Spinner and tie up some of both patterns.

Callibaetis CDC Biot Mayfly Spinner (John Berryman)

Callibaetis CDC Biot Mayfly Spinner

Hook:	Dry fly, e.g., Tiemco TMC 100, sizes 14 and 16
Thread:	Tan
Underwing:	White CDC, spinner-style
Overwing:	Brown Dar-lon or Z-lon
Tail:	White Betts' tail fibers
Abdomen:	Light tan turkey biot

Both of these flies imitate mayflies that are common in several of the waters that Brad and I fish regularly. The massive Callibaetis hatches that occur in Colorado lakes and reservoirs are of just as much interest to carp as they are to trout. Use different hook sizes and colors to tie imitations of the mayflies that are most common in your waters. When large numbers of insects are emerging, having the right mayfly dry flies and emergers in your fly box can result in terrific dry-fly action for carp.

Adult Damselfly (John Berryman)

Adult Damselfly

Hook:	Wet fly or nymph, 2X-heavy, e.g., Tiemco TMC 3769, size 10
Thread:	Blue
Tail:	Braided poly cord, colored blue with permanent marker, optional stripes or speckles with black permanent marker
Hackle:	Grizzly or white, tied to back of fly
Underbody:	Peacock blue Antron dubbing
Overbody:	1/8″ closed-cell foam, blue or colored blue with permanent marker

Brad and I agree that any opportunity to cast to clooping carp should be treated as an event and that the opportunity to cast adult damsels to surface-feeding carp is something even more special. Brad is deadly when carp are taking adult damsels. Making a shrewd assessment of their direction of travel, he casts in front of the cloopers and waits until the fish intercept the fly. The action dilemma then comes into play. Should he give the fly some action or not? If the fish are going to miss the fly and they don't appear too spooky, he'll risk a twitch. If they look like they're going to intercept the fly, he does nothing.

On a final note, an adult damselfly imitation is also a fine fly to cast to clooping carp when you're not completely sure what they're eating. Many times, an adult damsel imitation will provoke a strike even if you don't see damselflies on the water.

Dandelion or Thistle Seed (John Berryman)

Dandelion or Thistle Seed

Hook:	Wet fly or nymph, 1XL, e.g., Tiemco TMC 3761, sizes 8-16
Thread:	White
Body:	Brown Super Floss, as seed stem
Hackle:	White or grizzly, as seed tuft

We were serious about seed flies. This fly is designed to hang vertically in the film, supported by the hackle, in the same way the tuft supports a dandelion or thistle seed. This fly is a good choice for cloopers that show a preference for the salad bar; grass carp, in particular, seem to like it. You may need to use other colors to imitate seed types in your area. For the realism fanatics in the audience, a small ball of dubbing can be added at the bend of the hook to imitate the seed itself.

CDC Cottonwood Seed (John Berryman)

CDC Cottonwood Seed

Hook:	Shrimp/caddis pupa, e.g., Tiemco TMC 2487, sizes 12 and 14
Thread:	White
Wing:	4-6 white CDC fibers, as seed tuft

Brad and I started out using tiny balls of cotton tied on small hooks to imitate cottonwood seeds. Other anglers we talked to simply used basic dry-fly patterns tied in white. While we took occasional fish using these flies, it wasn't until we began using CDC that we were really able to consistently take carp that were feeding on these fuzzy seeds. We learned that carp can be just as selective with respect to plant food as they can be with insects. This is the best imitation of a cottonwood seed that we've found to date.

Terrestrials

Terrestrial patterns are an excellent choice from late spring through early fall. At these times of the year, when the naturals are most likely to be in the water, carp readily take hopper, beetle, ant, and cricket patterns. When conditions are right, a pond can be covered with flying ants and twenty-fish days are possible. You'll catch every one of those fish on surface strikes.

Taking advantage of this bonanza means doing your best to track the erratic movements of rising carp. A lot of the time you'll be wrong, and you need to be prepared to pick up your fly and cast again. Running the risk of spooking these skittish fish is part of the game, as is casting until your fly and presentation finally suits a carp's fancy.

Ant (John Berryman)

Ant

Hook:	Dry fly, e.g., Tiemco TMC 100, sizes 14 and 16
Thread:	Black
Body:	Black Antron
Hackle:	Black

As we've said, you'll need to determine where those clooping carp are headed and get this fly in front of them. This pattern is useful when rains wash ants into the lake. We tend to fish this fly without any action.

Befus' Flying Ant (John Berryman)

Befus' Flying Ant

Hook: Dry fly, e.g., Tiemco TMC 100, sizes 12-16
Thread: Black
Body: Black Antron
Legs: Black Krystal Flash
Wing: Pearl Saltwater Flashabou

Flights of flying ants can occur anytime during warm weather. When flying ants are on the water, they're usually the prime target of all species of fish, not just carp. Ants are always a preferred food, and at no time are they more available than during these flights. Because this fly represents an insect that is typically struggling when it ends up in the water, we use twitches during the retrieve.

Whitlock Beetle (John Berryman)

Whitlock Beetle

Hook:	Dry fly, e.g., Tiemco TMC 100, sizes 14-18
Thread:	Black
Back:	Black elk hair
Body:	Pearly green Flashabou
Head:	Black elk hair
Legs:	Black elk hair
Indicator:	Orange egg yarn

During the summer months, beetles blunder into the drink with some regularity. These fellows don't struggle so much as they try to slowly walk their way back to dry land across the film. A still presentation works fine, but if you move the fly, a very slow, steady, inch-by-inch retrieve is appropriate.

Whitlock Hopper (John Berryman)

Whitlock Hopper

Hook:	Nymph or streamer, 3XL, e.g., Tiemco TMC 5263, sizes 4-12
Thread:	Pale yellow
Extended body:	Light elk
Underwing:	Pale yellow deer hair
Wing:	Dark mottled turkey quill
Legs:	Yellow-dyed grizzly hackle stem
Indicator:	Orange egg yarn
Head:	Natural deer hair

The Whitlock Hopper and the Whitlock Cricket that follows are essential patterns for the carp flyfisher. Tips on fishing these patterns are given in the information for the Whitlock Cricket.

Whitlock Cricket (John Berryman)

Whitlock Cricket

Hook:	Nymph or streamer, 3XL, e.g., Tiemco TMC 5263, sizes 6-14
Thread:	Black
Tail:	Black deer hair and brown poly yarn
Body:	Brown poly yarn and black hackle, palmered
Wing:	Black turkey quill
Legs:	Black turkey quill section, knotted
Collar:	Black deer hair
Head:	Black deer hair

Hoppers and crickets wind up in the water quite often and, like ants, they seem to be a favorite snack of every fish species, including carp. We fish these flies two ways, often on the same retrieve. When a hopper or cricket lands in the water, it's dry and often attempts to escape with vigorous kicks of its strong hind legs. We use short, fairly sharp twitches to imitate this behavior.

Rather than freeing the insect, this struggling often has the opposite effect—the hopper or cricket breaks though the surface film and drowns. Allowing the fly to float quietly in the water imitates the natural in this situation (obviously). So, many times we'll cast a hopper and, after the water has settled, give the fly some twitches. Sooner or later, we'll get a bit carried away and the fly, like the natural, will break through the film. We let these drowned flies soak for a while. Often, a carp that was reluctant to come to the surface for a kicking hopper will happily accept a drowned one.

Stewart's Spider (John Berryman)

Stewart's Spider

Hook:	Dry fly, e.g., Tiemco TMC 100 sizes 12-16
Thread:	Chartreuse
Underbody:	Chartreuse thread
Hackle:	Medium dun
Head:	Chartreuse thread

The Spider and the Woolly Worm that follows are great generic patterns for carp. They often work in the toughest carp situations.

Chartreuse Woolly Worm (John Berryman)

Chartreuse Woolly Worm

Hook: Dry fly, e.g., Tiemco TMC 100, sizes 12-16
Thread: Chartreuse
Body: Chartreuse rabbit fur, dubbed, or extra-
               small chartreuse chenille
Tail: Red saddle hackle fibers
Hackle: Grizzly hen hackle

We use these flies to entice non-feeding cruising or stationary carp. Light-wire hooks are used for both flies so they'll sink slowly and naturally. With cruisers, the name of the game is once again to estimate direction of travel and to cast so that the slowly sinking fly will intercept the path of the carp. Slow strips can reduce the speed of the sink and can be used to move the fly into the path of the fish.

With stationary fish, a cast directly above the snout of the fish seems to work best. For some reason, perhaps because it may be difficult for them to see the leader, this tactic works particularly well for stationary fish that are facing the angler.

Other Flies

The flies in this eclectic assortment may surprise you. Some come from saltwater flyfishing, while others are borrowed from bass and pike flyfishing. All of them share something in common, however—they catch carp.

Agent Orange (John Berryman)

Agent Orange

Hook:	Saltwater, e.g., Tiemco TMC 811S, sizes 6 and 8
Thread:	Orange
Weight:	Lead wire
Body:	Orange chenille
Wing:	Orange Krystal Flash with grizzly hackle tips on each side
Eyes (optional):	Extra-small bead chain

This fly was designed for bonefish, but it just so happens that this little fellow is also deadly for carp! While it's most effective in stillwater, it will also take carp in moving water. When tied with bead-chain eyes, it bounces right along the bottom where carp root. In muddy areas, the eyes stir up little clouds of mud, much like those produced by a fleeing crayfish.

Back Swimmer (John Berryman)

Back Swimmer

Hook:	Straight-eye dry fly, e.g., Tiemco TMC 101, sizes 14 and 16
Thread:	Black
Body:	Silver oval plastic bead
Back:	Black marker or fabric paint
Legs:	Black turkey biot

Back swimmers are strong, if erratic, swimmers. We retrieve these flies with short, hard strips. This causes the fly to dart and approach the surface, imitating the natural. The Back Swimmer is an excellent fly in spring and fall when other insects are not abundant.

Befus' Epoxy Scud (John Berryman)

Befus' Epoxy Scud

Hook:	Wet fly or nymph, 1XL, e.g., Tiemco TMC 3761, sizes 10-18
Thread:	To match body
Tail:	Lemon wood duck (or substitute)
Shellback:	Krystal Flash to match body, epoxy coated
Body:	Olive, rust, gray, tan, or orange Scintilla Dubbing
Eyes:	Spotted with fine-tip permanent marker

Scuds are eaten by virtually all fish, and carp are no exception. Brad was fishing for carp in some gravel-pit ponds one early April. He noticed large numbers of carp creating quite a commotion. Some other anglers were casting to the carp and, as Brad watched, they caught perhaps twenty carp in the next hour. Their secret? A large orange scud with a split-shot clamped about ten inches above the fly.

Now that we know the effectiveness of scuds, we cast them to carp regularly. Typically, we cast the fly a foot or so in front of a carp and allow it to sink slowly. Often, the carp will literally pounce on the fly! Scuds are especially effective around weed beds. Short, erratic strips seem to work best.

Bar 'Bou Face (John Berryman)

Barr 'Bou Face

Hook:	Nymph, 3XL, e.g., Tiemco TMC 200R, sizes 8-12
Thread:	Black or to match fly color
Head:	Brass bead
Tail:	Olive rabbit strip, pierced, passed over point, and tied down at head
Body:	Olive marabou fibers topped with 2 or 3 strands of gold Flashabou
Collar:	Olive rabbit fur, dubbed

John Barr's Barr 'Bou Face is one of the most versatile flies in the angler's arsenal. Tied big and bushy, pike and largemouth take them eagerly. Tied small and sparse, trout, panfish, and carp take them just as enthusiastically. Stripped fast, a small 'Bou Face can imitate a swimming nymph or a minnow. Stripped more slowly, it becomes a seductively undulating leech imitation. And fished dead, the 'Bou Face is a good imitation of drifting aquatic plants. Though this version is tied in olive, we also tie them in black for leeches, brown or rust for nymphs and swimming crayfish, and gray, natural rabbit, and white for baitfish.

Reynolds' 'Poxy 'Dad (John Berryman)

Reynolds' 'Poxy 'Dad

Hook:	Saltwater, e.g., Tiemco TMC 811S, sizes 6 and 8
Antennae:	Stripped grizzly hackle vein
Mouth Parts:	Tan rabbit fur
Eyes:	Mono
Body:	Tan rabbit fur, dubbed
Legs:	Brown saddle hackle
Shell:	Tan, olive, dark brown, or rust Bugskin spotted with marker, epoxy coated
Claws:	Tan, olive, dark brown, or rust Bugskin spotted with marker, epoxy coated

I developed the 'Poxy 'Dad to create a realistic fly that can be tied fairly quickly and easily. The 'Poxy 'Dad and the Whitlock NearNuff Crayfish, described next, are both important patterns for the carp flyfisher.

Whitlock NearNuff Crayfish (John Berryman)

Whitlock NearNuff Crayfish

Hook:	Nymph or streamer, 3XL, e.g., Tiemco TMC 5263, sizes 6-10
Antennae:	Pumpkin Silly Legs, black Span-flex, and pearl Krystal Flash
Claws:	Tan grizzly hen saddle tips colored with fabric paint
Eyes:	Small mono
Legs:	Tan grizzly hen saddle hackle, palmered
Body:	Tannish-rust rabbit fur, dubbed
Rib:	Fine gold wire
Weight:	Extra-small lead eyes, painted brown with fabric paint
Tail:	Tannish-rust rabbit fur

When they're feeding over gravel or small rocks, you can figure that carp are looking for one of their favorite foods, crayfish. Whitlock's NearNuff Crayfish has produced well for me, particularly in creeks and rivers. It sinks quickly, stays on the bottom, and has enough motion to appear very lifelike. After the fly has sunk, I like to give it six or seven short, slow strips, followed by an occasional short, quick strip. Often, this will jump-start sullen carp. Weight is critical for all crayfish patterns. To be effective, the fly needs to be heavy enough to be crawled and bounced along the bottom.

Marabou Clouser Minnow (John Berryman)

Marabou Clouser Minnow

Hook: Saltwater, e.g., Tiemco TMC 811S, sizes 4-8
Thread: Brown, 3/0
Eyes: Small or extra-small lead eyes, painted
Wing: Olive or rusty brown marabou

The Marabou Clouser is a very productive bottom-bouncer. Tied in olive, it's the closest thing to a "vegetation fly" that Brad and I tie. At one time or another, Marabou Clousers have produced carp for us virtually everywhere: in heavy vegetation, over muddy bottoms, and even over rubble bottoms in gin-clear water. The wariest of carp seem to be seduced by the undulating motion of the marabou.

Marabou Clousers can be very effective on cruising carp. Many times the cruisers will inhale the fly on the drop. Strikes can be very subtle and paying close attention to your leader or the end of your fly line is crucial. Although olive and rusty brown have been the most productive colors for Brad and me, don't let this stop you from trying some of your own ideas.

No-Name Baitfish (John Berryman)

No-Name Baitfish

Hook:	Nymph, 3XL, e.g., Tiemco TMC 200R, sizes 4-12
Thread:	Gray, 3/0
Body:	Silver Sparkle Braid
Belly:	White Icelandic sheep hair
Back:	Gray Icelandic sheep hair
Eyes:	Red or gold Prizm Tape, epoxy coated

Because it's light, the No-Name Baitfish works well in very shallow water. Its soft, full wing causes the fly to land gently, so that schooling baitfish aren't spooked. We use white and gray most often, but you should feel free to vary colors to imitate local species of baitfish.

There you have it, our basic carp fly box. The flies presented here are a good foundation that we hope you'll use to build your own selection of carp flies. We also hope that, as you begin to observe their habits and catch carp, you'll take the time to develop new flies just for carp.

SIX

PRESENTATION

In this chapter, we're going to talk about presentations, and perhaps the first thing we'd better do is define what we mean when we use that word. We'll use the word "presentation" in two ways. One way is probably familiar to you.

Presentation: The set of actions taken by a flyfisher when casting a fly to a fish. These can include fly selection, positioning before the cast is made, where the fly is cast in relation to the fish, control of the depth and sink rate of the fly, and retrieval strategies and methods.

The second way we'll use this word is different from the way you may have seen it used in the past.

Presentation: A combination of attributes displayed by a fish that provide the angler with a set of clues for determining what the angler should do in response. The attributes displayed by the fish include general behavior (e.g., cruising, tailing, rooting, and clooping in the case of carp) and location in the water (deep or shallow, in open water or holding tightly to cover).

These two kinds of "presentation" are closely interrelated, of course. If you fail to understand the presentation—the fishing opportunity—offered by the fish, it's likely that the fish will fail to respond to your presentation.

This concept is important when fishing for any fish, but it is absolutely crucial when casting flies to carp. A carp can be found almost anywhere in a lake, from shallow bays to open water, can be doing almost anything, from purposeful swimming to erratic clooping, and can be eating almost anything, from cottonwood seeds to crawdads. Essentially, you must observe the fish and, based on what you see, determine the correct presentation.

This is an interactive process, and the carp respond with a take, a follow, a refusal, a spook, or no movement at all. Any nonstriking response is an additional presentation of information from the fish to the angler. You should use this information to refine or change your next presentation to the fish.

Carp require you to use a greater variety of presentations than any game fish we know of.

We've already discussed carp behavior briefly, but to understand that behavior and plan an appropriate presentation in return, you must also take into account the setting in which you observe the carp. Broadly speaking, there are two settings, shallow water and deeper, open-water situations.

Shallow Water

Because of the limitations of our tackle, because most fish, including carp, do the bulk of their feeding in shallow water, and because shallow water offers the best opportunity to see and stalk carp, we think you'll do the majority of your carp flyfishing in shallow water. It's our favorite kind of carp flyfishing, and depending on what sort of behavior the carp is presenting, it can be the most productive kind. Here are the presentations carp make in shallow water and what you should try in response.

Shallow-water Tailers

- Individual or groups of fish
- Purposeful, consistent tailing
- Likely to be feeding selectively
- Spooky during calm days
- Odds of success: excellent

Tailers are carp that are feeding along the bottom in a head-down posture. Because they're feeding in shallow water, from time to time their tails protrude from the water. A tailing carp is a feeding carp!

You'll find them in both clear and cloudy water. They move with purpose and their direction of travel is reasonably easy to determine. While they're often very selective, this is balanced by the fact that since they move slowly, it's possible to place the fly accurately with respect to the fish. Because these fish are feeding consistently and systematically, they seem to be focused on what they're doing and are somewhat less spooky than other carp.

Angler's Response

We have developed three basic responses to this presentation by the carp. You should try them in the following order.

First, we cast slightly in front of the fish (one to three feet—experimentation is required) and allow the fly to sink. When this response works, the fish moves forward, inspects the fly, and dips its head to take it.

If the first response doesn't work, we cast again and try a short strip or two to get the carp's attention. We watch for the carp to move forward and take the fly.

Finally, without lining the carp or any others nearby, we cast beyond the target fish and allow the fly to sink. Then we slowly, gently strip the fly back toward the fish so that the fly intercepts its path.

Initial Fly Selection

Soft bottoms: San Juan Worm, damselfly nymphs, Prince or Hare's Ear nymphs, or Clouser Swimming Nymph (size and color determined by experimentation and local food availability).

Gravel and rock bottoms: crayfish patterns or larger nymphs, such as Princes, Hare's Ears, or stoneflies. (Be sure to try stoneflies in moving water.)

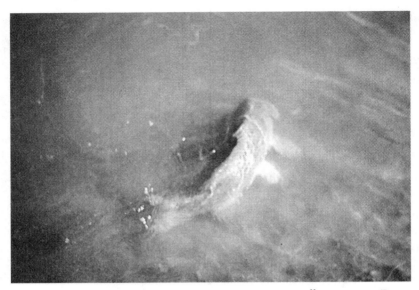

Rooters can be among the most aggressive carp you will encounter. (Barry Reynolds)

Shallow-water Rooters

- Often individual fish
- Searching, erratic behavior
- Constant motion
- Sporadic feeding
- Not as selective
- Odds of success: excellent

Rooters feed actively and can be among the most aggressive carp you will encounter. Most often seen individually, these fish are rooting on the bottom and their behavior is characterized by a sudden, sporadic dipping of the head as the carp dives to nab something.

While they often move as slowly and systematically as tailers, they can also cover the bottom fairly quickly. These fish are more difficult to see than tailers, which means that a clever angler will take a moment to scan the water before casting to avoid lining a closer fish.

Angler's Response

There are two responses that we like to use for rooters, and we select between them based upon what the fish are telling us.

When rooters are moving slowly, the tactics described for tailers can be used successfully. Most often, because these fish are feeding aggressively, allowing the fly to sit motionless will work fine. If the fly is passed by, we try again, perhaps casting closer this time, or we switch flies.

When a rooter is moving at a faster clip, we first try to determine the fish's general direction of travel. We then cast farther in front of the fish than we would for a slowly moving fish. Again, because they are feeding aggressively, it's not necessary to give the fly much action.

Initial Fly Selection

Because rooting carp are feeding on whatever they happen across, just about any fly may work. This is one time where a look at a handful of muck or the underside of a rock or two may be a good idea so that you can get an idea of what food is available.

Soft Bottoms: scud, Hare's Ear, Prince, and damselfly nymphs, San Juan Worm, Barr 'Bou Face, and Clouser Swimming Nymph.

Gravel and Rock Bottoms: crayfish patterns and larger sizes of the same nymphs.

Shallow-water Mudders

- Groups of fish
- Moving slowly and systematically
- Mud provides cover
- Likely to be selective feeders
- Odds of success: good

Mudders are essentially rooters traveling in groups and feeding over soft bottoms. Next to cloopers, they're probably the easiest carp to spot because of the muddy water they create. Typically, these carp are mudding because they have found a rich feeding ground. They usually travel slowly and feed consistently, and their direction of travel is reasonably predictable. As an added plus, the cloud of mud produced by their feeding gives them cover, so mudders are among the least spooky carp. They're usually the most approachable of all carp in shallow water.

Angler's Response

Finding the fish is no problem. Determining where the fish are going is usually no problem. And since all sorts of organisms live in soft bottoms, fly selection is generally not as critical as it is with other types of carp you'll see, although the fly must be fished on or near the bottom. However, getting your fly noticed in clouds of mud and agitated detritus can be a problem.

We've evolved two responses to this situation and we use them equally often, with roughly the same success.

First, cast into the clear water in front of the moving cloud of mud. The theory is that the fly will be easy for the lead fish to spot, and since we already know that the mudders are feeding, it is quite likely to be picked up. It's also somewhat easier to detect a take in this situation. The disadvantage here is that the thrashing of the lead fish when it's hooked can spook the rest of the group.

Our second response is to cast into the heart of the mud. In this case, the odds of detecting a strike are less. In the haze of mud, it's also probably more difficult for a carp to spot your fly. On the other hand, in this confused setting, we think carp may be more likely to sample an unfamiliar offering, if only because they can't inspect it visually. Finally, you may be able to hook and land a carp without breaking up the group.

Initial Fly Selection

Any subsurface fly will probably work. A bead head or a bit of flesh may help get the fly noticed.

Shallow-water Cloopers
- Likely to be in groups but occasional loners
- Movements random, difficult to predict
- Likely to be feeding selectively
- Very spooky
- Odds of success: good to excellent

Shallow-water cloopers are not just among the spookiest of all carp, they are among the spookiest of all fish. You can put these surface-feeding carp down with a fly line, the splashy arrival of a fly, your shadow, or an impure thought. They're typically found in groups when the density of food on the surface of the water is quite high. This food can be either plant matter or insects, but there must be lots of it! It takes a great deal of food to persuade a cautious carp to expose itself on the surface. Unlike surface-feeding trout, which usually rise individually and somewhat erratically, clooping carp are usually tightly grouped and move systematically across the water (though their actual course may be very difficult to predict) as they sweep up seeds, ants, midges, or other insects.

Angler's Response
First and foremost, be quiet! Their consistent feeding may lull you into believing that these fish are too busy to pay attention to you, but nothing could be further from the truth.

Next, try to determine the base course of the cloopers. This can be difficult, since when the surface is covered with food, carp can move in any direction and still feed successfully.

Finally, try to get a sense of the size and shape of the group. This is probably most important of all, because if you frighten one fish with your line or leader or hook a fish in the midst of its fellows, your precious cloopers are likely to vanish in a heartbeat. Even though the sight of cloopers makes every carp aficionado's heart race, we recommend taking a deep breath and spending a bit of time to make sure that you select a fish from the fringes of the group.

Initial Fly Selection

The bad news is that we've found cloopers to be the most selective of all carp. The good news is that, since what they're eating is on the surface, you can usually identify the food and match it. If they're eating cottonwood seeds, show them your cottonwood seed imitation. If they're eating adult damselflies, that's what you should cast. There are two situations that may puzzle you, however, and you'll need to make some adjustments.

The first situation occurs when the carp seem to be eating nothing. This usually means they're feeding on midges that you're having difficulty seeing and a small midge pattern, such as a Griffith's Gnat, may be the ticket.

The second situation occurs when your nicest mayfly dun or adult damsel is rejected even though you're sure you've identified what the carp are feeding on. At such times, it's likely that the carp are taking emergers. Often, a carp with a critical eye that has rejected a dry fly can be persuaded to hit an emerger.

Shallow-water Hell Raisers

- Individual fish
- Breaching, splashing, leaping
- Occurs when carp pursue baitfish and during spawning
- Odds of success: fair to good if feeding; poor to fair during spawn

Shallow-water hell raisers are exactly that: carp that are making a spectacle of themselves by leaping, splashing, and thrashing in the shallows. These fish seem utterly oblivious to the dangers they may face by drawing attention to themselves.

Often, there is a reason for this, particularly in the spring when carp are spawning. As you might expect, spawning fish are usually not very interested in your fly—they have other things in mind. But at other times, these hell raisers are carp that are smashing through schools of baitfish and they're a very good target for a small streamer.

Hell raisers make a spectacle of themselves by leaping and splashing in the shallows. (Brad Befus)

The numbers of hell raisers present will help you tell the difference between spawners and baitfish feeders. If there is a general riot taking place in the shallows, with many fish taking part, chances are you're seeing courtship and mating behavior. But if just a few carp (or even a single carp) seem to be misbehaving, you may be seeing predation on baitfish. Additional confirmation is provided during the unfortunately rare occasions when the hell raisers move in a consistent direction, trailing a school of baitfish and feeding as they go.

Angler's Response

Because the course of hell raisers is usually difficult to predict and the behavior itself is often sporadic, it's unlikely that you'll be deliberately fishing for hell raisers. Usually, a hell raiser will present itself as an accidental target.

Initial Fly Selection

If you're already using a streamer, try it first, but if you've been casting a Wiggle Bug to some cruisers, go ahead and cast it to a hell raiser if you spot one. After dashing around after baitfish, carp become quite aggressive. A feeding hell raiser is likely to belt anything that moves.

The baitfish that carp pursue tend to be on the small, weak, slow side, and when hell raisers are feeding consistently enough to warrant tying on a streamer, we tend to fish small, soft streamers possessing the translucency often present in very young fish. No-Name Baitfish and Clouser Minnows are good choices.

Shallow-water Cruisers

- Groups or individuals
- Moving rapidly, searching
- Challenging to hit
- Odds of success: good

Shallow-water cruisers present yet another carp enigma to the angler. These are groups of fish or individual fish that are moving purposefully, and their direction of travel is more consistent than it is with tailers, rooters, or cloopers. What is difficult to determine is what they're actually doing. As far as we're concerned, that can only be determined by casting to them. At times, cruisers are quite willing to take advantage of a feeding opportunity. At other times, seemingly fixed on whatever mission they are involved in, they resolutely ignore the most seductive of offerings. Because their direction of travel is reasonably predictable, you can usually determine where to cast, although this can still be challenging.

Angler's Response

As is so often the case, the key to shallow cruisers is observation by the angler. The things to look for are:

1. Where the fish are going. Determine their direction of travel and quietly position yourself or direct your casts so that you can target individual fish without lining other members of the group.

2. Behavior. This is a little more tricky. Are the fish staying together in a tight group or are individuals leaving the group

from time to time? Are they swimming purposefully, without interruption? (Not so good—these fish may have traveling, not eating, on their minds.) Or do they seem willing to investigate the bottom or clumps of weeds occasionally? (Better—these fish may be willing to dine on something tasty if they have the opportunity to do so.)

Above all, keep watching. Sometimes, your cruisers are just that: fish that are moving from one place to another. You'll get a crack at them as they pass by, but if you want to cast to these fish repeatedly, you'll just have to follow them. But other times, cruising fish are really the circulators that we alluded to in Chapter 2. They're likely to be moving in a rough circle in the deeper portion of a bay or close to a drop-off or other cover. Individuals or groups of fish will leave the main group from time to time to forage in shallower water, where they are more available.

If you find circulators, you can quietly make your way back to shallower water and use tailer, rooter, or mudder tactics as appropriate, going after feeding fish that temporarily leave the main group. Or, you can make a cast or two each time the group happens by. Cast to individual fish on the fringes of the group. You don't want to break up this nice, predictable group of fish.

Initial Fly Selection

When casting to cruisers, you're seeking to accomplish two things. First, you're trying to place your fly where it will be noticed by a moving fish. This generally means using a weighted fly of some kind. Often, you will have little time from when you spot the fish to when you must make a cast.

Second, you're trying to make that offering more appealing than whatever else is on the carp's mind. Usually, this means using a fly that's flashier and sometimes a bit larger than usual. For smaller flies, Epoxy Scuds, Agent Oranges, and small Bead-Head Princes work well. If it takes a juicier fly to get the carp's attention, we like to use Clouser Swimming Nymphs, Wiggle Bugs, and Barr 'Bou Faces.

Shallow-water Stationary

- Individuals and groups of fish, sunbathing
- Little or no motion
- Can be aggressive toward fly
- Odds of success: fair to good

Are they beach bums? Are they sleeping off a good meal? We don't know. We do know that these fish aren't actively feeding and that they're found both as individuals and groups, sometimes in ridiculously shallow water with portions of their backs protruding from the surface. Almost always seen when the water is dead calm and the sun is bright, these fish can be found in both clear and cloudy water. This behavior is more common in the spring, as the sun warms shallow waters.

Overall, we rate these sunbathers as a 50/50 proposition. For every beach bum that grabs your fly, another will either ignore it or flee for deeper water. When these fish are found in groups, we select our targets carefully to minimize the chances of lining other sunbathers or startling them if the carp strikes or spooks.

Angler's Response

The key to catching the interest of these sleepyheads is presenting them with the fly from a variety of angles and being willing to experiment with fly patterns until something catches their attention. Because the water will usually be dead calm, stealth is as important as casting accuracy. We usually begin by casting about three feet from the fish and slowly move closer with our casts. We also quietly change position so that we can present the fly to the fish from different angles.

Because we're trying to get the attention of a listless fish, a jiggle or a twitch of the fly is appropriate. As we cast closer, we're likely to try smaller flies. Overall, we always consider our chances spotty. If the first carp we cast to spooks or refuses to pay any attention to our fly, we don't despair. We just look around for another fish and give it a try.

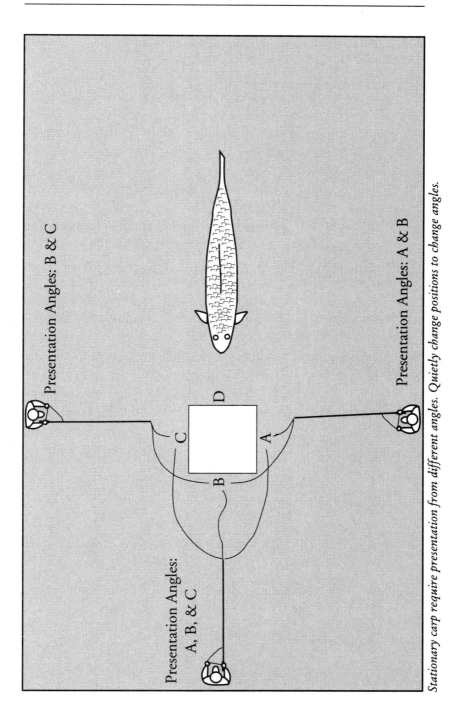

Stationary carp require presentation from different angles. Quietly change positions to change angles.

Initial Fly Selection

With respect to flies for shallow, stationary fish, there are two basic options.

First, you can go small and subtle. Tie on a little Hare's Ear Nymph, for example, and present it close to the stationary fish, working it to within inches of its nose. Your intent is to present the carp, in a non-threatening way, with a little morsel of something that's easy for it to eat.

Or, you can go big and beautiful. Present the carp with something quite a bit larger, such as a Wiggle Bug, dragonfly nymph, or Barr 'Bou Face. Give the fish something big and flashy enough to get its attention—something that represents a meal large enough to convince the fish to move. If you're going big and beautiful, place the fly far enough away that it doesn't frighten the fish.

We usually start with the small-and-subtle approach. If we strike out, we use the big-and-beautiful approach, casting perhaps three feet from the fish. We move closer with successive casts until the carp either takes the fly or shows signs of nervousness. If the fish begins looking spooky, we rest it; there's no point spooking an entire group of snoozers because we annoyed one fish excessively.

Regardless of which approach we use, we try to keep the fly in front of these fish for as long as possible, drifting something yummy in front of a carp long enough to allow its greed to overcome its tendency to continue napping. This is, therefore, a good application for unweighted flies, such as scuds, Prince and Hare's Ear nymphs, and Wiggle Bugs.

Because you're trying to catch the attention of a fish that's not actively feeding, it's also a good time to consider flies with a bit of flash or glitter. A slowly sinking Woolly Bugger or Barr 'Bou Face, with marabou breathing seductively and highlighted with a bit of Krystal Flash or Flashabou, can be deadly.

Open Water

As you might expect, the distinction between shallow water and open water is often blurred. When we speak of open-water carp,

Small-and-subtle or big-and-beautiful, keep your fly in front of the carp. (Barry Reynolds)

we're talking about carp that are in deep water where they don't have ready access to cover. Because of this, we think you'll find open-water carp even more spooky than shallow-water carp. Speaking broadly, these fish are more difficult to catch and you'll see fewer of them. But when you suddenly find your float tube surrounded by a group of cloopers or you happen across a monster carp sunbathing in deep water, you should take advantage of the opportunity.

Open-Water Cloopers

- Likely to be in groups
- Movements random, difficult to predict
- Likely to be feeding selectively
- Extremely spooky
- Odds of success: good to excellent

If you think shallow-water cloopers are spooky, wait until you meet open-water cloopers. Exposed and far from cover, they will vanish at the slightest disturbance. If you can maintain stealth, avoid lining members of the group, and plan your casts carefully, they're just as willing to accept the appropriate surface fly as are shallow-water cloopers.

Incidentally, open-water cloopers typically move a bit faster than a float-tuber can. While trailing them in a belly boat is great exercise, it's usually better to wait for the fish to come to you.

Angler's Response

Determine their course, as you would with shallow-water cloopers. Choose your target just as carefully, or more so. Finally, remember that these open-water cloopers are even more skittish than shallow-water cloopers.

Initial Fly Selection

You should follow the same advice we gave for shallow-water cloopers. Identify what the fish are feeding on and match it. Invisible hatches are probably midges.

Open-Water Cruisers

- Likely to be in groups
- Moving purposefully at mid-speed
- Odds of success: fair (dependent on depth of fish)

The behavior these carp present is essentially the same as their shallow-water counterparts. While they are reasonable targets, their depth and speed can make casting to them difficult. The more shallow they are and the slower they're moving, the greater your odds of success.

Angler's Response

As with shallow-water cruisers, you must determine direction of travel and target individual fish to avoid spooking the whole group. Watch for fish leaving the group to feed.

Initial Fly Selection

We approach these fish just as we do cruisers in shallow water. Weighted flies that have color and flash are best. Additional weight may be required for deeper fish.

Open-Water Stationary, Shallow, Less Than Two Feet Deep

- Likely to be individuals, sunbathing
- Little or no motion
- Easily spooked
- Odds of success: poor to fair

Like their shallow-water counterparts, some of these fish are willing to take a look at a fly, while others will ignore everything you throw at them. They differ from shallow-water fish in that they're more likely to spook. Since the angler often comes upon these fish accidentally (usually spotting them from a float tube or a boat), it's easy to find yourself suddenly very close to a very large carp.

Angler's Response

Unfortunately, the only way to find out if you've found an active fish is to throw a fly reasonably close to it. Because these fish are very exposed, subtlety and care is in order. We like to cast beyond the fish and slowly retrieve past it from a variety of angles, working closer to the fish with each cast. Even if your sunbather is part of a group, the fish are often well separated, so spooking a whole collection of fish is usually not a worry. We cast progressively closer to these snoozers until they accept the fly or leave.

Initial Fly Selection

Once again, of primary concern is keeping the fly in front of the fish long enough to get its attention. Unweighted, comparatively flashy flies are our first choice: conventional Prince Nymphs, unweighted Wiggle Bugs and Barr 'Bou Faces, and unweighted

Hare's Ear Nymphs or scuds at times when extra subtlety seems warranted.

Open-Water Stationary, Two to Three Feet Deep
- Likely to be individuals
- Inactive
- Odds of success: poor to fair

This scenario is much like the one that precedes it, except that the fish are holding deeper. They're not actively feeding and are apparently aimless. We suspect that these carp may spend substantial periods of time basking in water that is warm enough to be pleasant and deep enough to offer some protection. Obviously these fish are difficult for the angler to spot, and overall we think this will be one of the rarer carp-fishing situations that you'll face. Generally, if we spot one of these fish and it appears to be a large one, we'll take the time to cast once or twice. If we see no response, we move on to other, hopefully better things.

Angler's Response
These can be especially frustrating fish to cast to. They're several feet deep, so a weighted fly would seem a good choice. But you still want to keep that fly in front of the fish for sufficient time to gain its attention. Weighted flies may sink too fast; unweighted flies may never get to an appropriate depth.

This is a situation that could drive an angler to drink were it not for the fact that we know from experience not to invest a lot of time on these carp. If we can't seem to get the fly to the fish, if the fish appears to be completely uninterested, we don't fight City Hall. We go somewhere else!

Initial Fly Selection
We approach this kind of fish the same way we do open-water stationary carp that are holding closer to the surface. Often we'll just try the fly we're already using, since we'll only be trying one or two casts.

Open-Water Hell Raisers

- Individual fish
- Breaching, splashing, leaping
- Unpredictable and sporadic
- Cause of behavior unknown
- Odds of success: poor to non-existent (Don't fall for these guys!)

Leaping, breaching, splashing in open water. We have no idea what these fish are doing. Possibly, they're tearing up open-water baitfish. On the other hand, they could be fleeing from a real or perceived predator. They may also be trying to shed a parasite. They could be sick, or it could be what passes for exuberance among carp. At any rate, the behavior appears to be sporadic, and we simply ignore it.

That's our "Angler's Response" to open-water hell raisers.

In summary, carp will present you with a variety of "looks"—more, we think, than any other freshwater fish. But they do play fair; with a bit of study, you can understand what the fish are saying to you and present them with an appropriate response.

We've now given you quite a few pieces of the carp puzzle. You have some general background information about carp, you know how to find the fish, you know what they eat, we've discussed some flies that will take carp, and in this chapter, we've talked about presentations that carp provide to you and some of the responses you might present to the carp. Next we'll add some information on tackle and then we'll integrate all this information.

SEVEN

FLY TACKLE FOR CARP

L et's admit it. Most of us flyfishers are equipment freaks, and when we decide to pursue a new species of fish, we not-so-secretly hope we'll need to buy something new. Unfortunately, while the carp is a worthy fish in every other respect, it falls pretty flat in the new equipment department. Although carp are strong, possess endurance, and are sometimes large, you probably already have the tackle necessary to handle them.

Rods

We both like nine-footers, and we typically use four- to six-weight gear. Lighter rods provide great entertainment if you're able to fish in small ponds or gravel pits where there's not much in the way of brush and snags. Five-, six-, or even seven-weight rods are better in the wind and will help you put the brakes on a frantic carp before it hangs you up in the brush. These heavier rods also cast weighted flies more efficiently, which becomes important if you find yourself fishing in deeper water.

If you have several rods, we'd recommend starting on the heavy side. That way, you can get a sense of the power of the fish you're likely to catch. If the carp run to three or four pounds, you'll have a blast with light gear. If you've found a mother lode of ten- to fifteen-pound fish, you'll be mighty grateful for every bit of fish-controlling power a heavier rod provides.

Although carp are strong and sometimes large, you probably already have the necessary tackle. (Brad Befus)

Reels

The backing capacity of your reel becomes important when fly-fishing for carp. Carp run great distances, particularly in moving water, and you'll likely be taken into your backing. We consider 100 yards of backing necessary. The backing, as you probably know, also increases the diameter of the spool and allows you to retrieve line faster. Since a carp will run back at you just as fast as it runs away from you, the ability to pick up line quickly is very important.

For most freshwater applications, drags serve to keep us from overrunning the reel when we strip off line. Rarely do freshwater anglers find need for the drag as a fish-fighting tool. Since we've compared carp to bonefish and promised you they'll take you into your backing, you've probably figured out that the drag on your carp reel needs to be tough and smooth. A smooth drag becomes crucial when casting small flies on light tippets to cloopers.

Lines and Backing

If you're a typical freshwater angler, whose backing generally serves only as a spool-expander, you may have become somewhat casual about the quality of the backing you use. Backing is cheap! If your backing has been on your reel for a while, we recommend replacing it. You will really need your backing with carp. At a minimum, check your line-to-backing and line-to-arbor knots or prepare to say good-bye to a good carp and an expensive fly line.

We're of the opinion that subdued fly-line colors work best. If you're on a budget, handling this issue can be as simple as using a gray or olive permanent marker to color the first twenty feet of your line. If you're in a position to acquire a carp line, you may want to consider a bonefish taper, since these lines are designed for a style of fishing that parallels carp fishing in many ways. We use a floating line for the vast majority of our carp fishing, and we strongly recommend weight-forward lines because of the heavy flies sometimes required.

Leaders and Tippets

For most of our carp fishing, we use seven-and-a-half-foot to nine-foot leaders with 1X to 3X tippets. In cloudy water, neither leader length or diameter seems to be especially critical. In clear water, though, carp are more discerning. And when fishing to cloopers with small midges or nymphs, leaders of twelve or even fifteen feet with tippets as light as 6X may be required.

As we've said before, it's important to pay attention to what the fish are telling you. If you're fishing in shallow, clear water and you're getting follows or refusals no matter what you cast to the fish, it's time to change to a lighter tippet. Likewise, if you cast to a group of cloopers and spook them, and the Fish Gods are kind enough to give you another chance at them, try a longer leader and lighter tippet when you cast again.

Because carp are often found in areas where deadfall, weeds, and other tippet-busting obstructions abound, you may want to use leader materials that offer more abrasion resistance than standard monofilament. The new fluorocarbon materials offer excellent knot-strength and much better abrasion resistance. As a plus, the smaller diameters of these new materials often allow them to slice through weeds better than monofilament, and overall they're less visible to fish.

Accessories

Flyfishing for carp requires about the same assortment of small, impossible-to-find-when-you-really-need-them gadgets used in trout fishing. Clippers, for trimming tippets and reducing dental bills, are nice, as are hemostats or a small pair of pliers for debarbing hooks. Incidentally, Brad and I use barbless hooks for carp. The carp's leathery lip holds a barbless fly very well, and barbless hooks are easier to remove from the fish (and from us).

We also find a net to be helpful at all times and crucial when we fish from a float tube or boat and in moving water when handling a carp may be difficult. Nets are also important when fishing for large carp. There's another device that you might want to consider that's known as the BogaGrip. This widget grasps the carp by the lower lip and permits you to lift the fish from the water without harming it or touching it with your hands. The BogaGrip

A net is helpful at times and crucial when fishing from a float tube. (Barry Reynolds)

also has a handy, built-in scale (available in thirty-pound capacity for the realist or fifty-pound capacity for the optimist).

Of course, split shot or moldable lead comes in handy and you'll need it most when you don't have it. Strike indicators and fly floatant are also good things to have around. During the summer months we usually wade wet in stillwater. We use waders early and late in the year and in moving water. It's pretty hard to go wrong with a name brand.

One item of equipment that is emphatically not a gadget is sunglasses. First, seeing someone flyfishing without eye protection frankly scares the hell out of us. Second, good polarized sunglasses help immeasurably in spotting fish. Your flies and your skill at presenting them mean nothing if you can't see the fish. You can avoid hours of frustration, as well as sight-threatening injuries and headaches from staring into glaring water, by using good polarized sunglasses.

A final item of equipment that we consider important is a small notebook. It's pretty hard to avoid learning a new lesson every time you flyfish for carp. Unfortunately, it's extremely easy to forget those lessons between trips. It takes just a minute to jot down a pearl of wisdom, an observation, or a note for future fly-tying experiments.

While we're sorry we're unable to help you assemble a giant list of carp-fishing "gotta-gets," we're also eager that you start fishing. And the next chapter will help you do just that.

EIGHT

PUTTING IT TOGETHER

We hope that the preceding portions of this book have been helpful. You now know something of the carp's natural and political histories. You know how to go about locating carp and you know what carp eat. You know what flies and presentation tactics Brad and I have found to be effective for carp. Hopefully, you've even taken a moment to check your fly line's backing. There remains but one thing for us to do. We need to put it all together where it really matters—on the water. Let's go carping!

Good morning. It's a great day for carp fishing, isn't it? It's warm enough to make wading pleasant, but there's just enough cloud cover and chop on the surface of the water to make the carp feel comfortable while foraging in shallow water. Spring has definitely arrived in the shallows, and there's new growth of vegetation, insects are emerging, and clouds of tiny fish are making their faltering way around. See that shallow bay over there? That's where we'll start fishing. When we've reached the shoreline, what do you think we should do first?

    a. Enter the water in a gravel area, so we don't stir up too much mud.
    b. Enter the water in a softer area that may offer more food to carp.
    c. Avoid stirring up the water at all and cast from shore.
    d. Have a cup of coffee and evaluate the situation.

The topography of the bottom will be much like the shore next to it. (Brad Befus)

Our answer would be "d." While we drink our coffee, we're going to formulate a plan. First of all, where's the sun? Carp spook at shadows, so we'll try to position ourselves so that any shadow we cast will be behind us.

Second, let's take a look at the topography, using the following pretty good rule: the topography of the bottom will, for some distance at least, be much like that of the shore next to it.

Look over there, where the shore slopes gently down to the water. Very likely, that's a flat, and it might be a good place for carp to feed. On the other side of the bay, where those bluffs come down to the water pretty steeply, the bottom is likely to drop off steeply, too. There might be water deep enough there for carp to suspend and sunbathe. Does a feeder creek enter the bay? If so, the creek channel will extend for some distance into the bay, providing a "highway" for traveling carp.

Those fertile flats look like a pretty good bet. Let's walk along the shore to the flats, positioning ourselves to avoid casting a shadow.

Once we're there, what should we do?

   a. Enter the water quietly.
   b. Make a cast or two along the shoreline.
   c. Do a little sunbathing ourselves while we watch the water.

Brad and I would opt for the last choice once again. Although we've found an initial target area, the need for planning and, above all, observing hasn't come to an end. If you haven't got your polarized sunglasses on, put them on. Now, let's quietly approach the water. There could be carp feeding right along the shoreline. Do you see any? Are there any insects coming off? Do you see any minnows or fry?

This might be a good time to grab a scoop of mud. What's slithering around in there? Whatever it is, odds are that carp will eat it. Do you have something like it in your vest?

Now it's time to scan the water farther out. Do you see carp? Let's take our time! As stealthy as we've been, we may still have spooked them and we may need to wait awhile for them to resume feeding. Look for a commotion in the shallows where carp might be rooting around. Watch for tails and nervous water. Try to spot shadows moving against the bottom. There! Was that a tail? Yes! And there's another—there's a bunch of them. Now what shall we do?

   a. Finally get our feet wet.
   b. Oh, no! More planning?

Sorry. Let's wait just a little bit longer and let's watch those tails for awhile. Are they showing up pretty consistently, indicating systematic feeding, or are they showing up sporadically, indicative of cruising carp that are stopping occasionally to feed? Which way are they going? Roughly, how fast are they moving? Can we determine the boundaries of the shoal? How deep is the water where the carp are feeding? And most tricky of all, if we spook the fish (either with our presence or by catching a fish), where is the cover they're likely to run to?

Determine the boundaries of the shoal before casting. (Robert Sweet)

Okay. They seem to be moving at a slow speed and their tails are in the air pretty consistently. They're feeders! Since they're moving slowly and the water is shallow, we probably won't need weight on the fly, nor will we need the flash that might be required if we were trying to get the attention of a group of cruisers. That little Hare's Ear might be just the ticket, so we'll try it first.

Let's enter the water over here. As nearly as we can tell, we'll be able to get far enough out into the water so a clean backcast is possible and, based on the direction they're traveling, the carp should swim right up to us if we don't spook them.

Good. We're wading quietly and not casting a shadow, and we're far enough ahead of the shoal so we won't spook them. Here they come! What next?

a. Place the fly out in front of the shoal.
b. What? More waiting?

Sorry, but let's wait. If we frighten or hook a lead fish, the rest of the shoal might panic. Let's keep watching and do the best we can to determine the boundaries of the shoal. We're after a fish we can cast to without lining the other fish. We may cast to a lead fish, if it's on our side of the shoal, or to another fish that's on the outskirts of the shoal, but we never want to cast across the group of carp.

Hey, what about that big carp over there? Yes, it's finally time to cast. A false cast or two, and you'll place your fly. But where?

a. Right in front of the fish.
b. About ten feet in front of the fish.
c. About three feet in front of the fish.
d. Dependent upon observation.

Despite all we've written so far, we'd be kidding you if we tried to make you believe that the answer to this one was anything other than "d." The window in which a carp feeds varies. The size of that window depends on several factors.

1. Clarity of water. Obviously, in clear water, a carp can see food at a greater distance.

2. The activity level of the carp. A carp that is feeding systematically may be somewhat more likely to move over to investigate food than a cruiser.

3. The nature of the food item. If a carp is feeding systematically on pretty large food, such as crayfish or larger nymphs, it may be quite willing to move ten feet or more for a nice, fat morsel. If it's feeding on smaller food, it may not be willing to move as far.

4. The amount of food available. If lots of food is present (often signaled by slowly moving, consistently feeding carp), odds are the fish will be less willing to move very far.

5. The speed of the fish. The faster the fish is traveling, the bigger the effective window and the more you will need to lead the fish.

Taking all these factors into account allows you to make a series of educated guesses. As a first approximation, Brad and I usually cast three to four feet in front of the fish. Okay, let's take a crack at one.

Oops! The fish was moving a little faster than we thought, and it swam right by your sinking fly. Notice how it shied away from your leader? What should we do now?

a. Pick up and cast again.
b. You're kidding. Not more waiting?

Yep, more waiting. Let the carp you missed pass your fly and wait just a bit longer. Is there a trailing carp? If there is, give the fly a twitch or two. If not, let's pick up and cast again. This time, let's lead that carp just a little more. Great!

Here it comes. It's getting close—give the fly a tiny twitch. It's spotted your fly! Down goes its head and up comes its tail. Did your fly line just move? Strike!

Look at it go! Say, that's a darned nice fish, seven or eight pounds maybe. Now, you're on your own! They *are* strong, aren't they?

Now that you've got the carp at your feet, you can easily remove the debarbed hook. Remember what we told you about schreckstoff? Handle the carp gently. If you can, just pluck the fly from its lip without removing the carp from the water. How about a quick photo before you release it?

Let's catch another one. Of course the shoal has scattered. That carp you caught kicked up quite a ruckus. But because you took a trailing fish, it's likely that the group wasn't frightened too badly and we'll see tails in a minute or two. Let's just stand here quietly, scan the water, and see what develops.

What's that? Out there, where the water is a bit deeper. Those shadows are moving, aren't they? They've moved out of sight, but let's watch for a bit. The carp are back, and they seem to be moving in the same direction. They're moving pretty quickly. They're in deeper water, so if they're feeding, it's pretty tough to tell. Do you know what sort of carp they are?

a. Cruisers.
b. Circulators.

Right. Since we're seeing these fish fairly regularly, it's most likely that they're circulators. As you no doubt remember, many times groups of these fish will leave the main shoal and come into the shallows to feed. The tailers you intercepted may well have been such a break-off group. Because of the commotion your carp kicked up, they may be a bit nervous right now. What do you think we should do?

a. Stand here quietly and see if some of the carp break off into the shallows.
b. Take a crack at the circulators.
c. Retreat in case our presence is keeping them from feeding.
d. All of the above.

Actually, we'd opt for "d," because this is one of the cases where it's possible to have your cake and eat it, too. Waiting a bit is always worthwhile; some of the fish might return to the shallows. While we wait, we can try to determine the route being taken by the circulators, just in case we decide to try to pick one off.

While we're waiting, we can also change flies. These fish are moving faster, they're in deeper water, and they're not actively feeding (as nearly as we can tell). It may take a bit of glitter to catch the attention of a circulator. Let's look in our fly boxes. Yeah. That Bead-Head Prince ought to do the trick.

There's a good reason to cast to these fish. Tactically, they're much like cruisers in that they're moving quickly and purposefully, and they're not actively feeding. But because they're circulating, we may get more than one chance at them. If nothing else, this will be good practice. Now, what about moving back?

This is a matter of the sun, casting position, and as always, the behavior of the fish. Do the carp seem to ease toward the shallows before and after they pass by and make a pretty wide swing around us? Or are they ignoring us? If they shy away, it may be time to move. But they really don't seem to be paying much attention to us. Let's not risk spooking them; we'll cast from here.

Yes, those carp are moving right along, aren't they? That means that we'll need to lead these fish more than we led the tailers. And let's remember something: the lead we give the fish is not the same as the active window. Think about that for a moment. The lead is the amount of distance you cast in front of the fish so that your fly will arrive in the carp's window at the right time. Therefore, we may need to lead a circulator (or cruiser) by, say, six feet to be able to have our fly arrive in the carp's three-foot active window. Got it?

And what about the size of that window? Once again, this is to some extent dependent on water clarity and the overall mood of the fish. Because these fish are purposeful and not actively feeding, we usually consider the window to be smaller, perhaps two feet.

There! See that carp, the one that's traveling pretty much alone? Let's try it.

Good cast. It's a shame the fish was moving so fast. Let it pass, then pick up and cast again, giving the fish a bit more lead this time. Great, your fly was right at the carp's depth and two feet in front of it when it swam by. But it ignored your fly. Wait a minute, here comes one of its buddies, and it looks like the fish is going to pass right over your fly! Wait for it. When it's about two feet away, give your fly a twitch.

Yeah, those fish are probably blind. Now, we've got a choice. We can continue to cast various flies at these fish, or we can look around for something more exciting. We might spend some time watching these fish in hopes they'll decide to feed, but as you've just seen, these can be pretty fickle fish, and we usually try to find some more willing customers.

Hey, what was that? Out there, in the middle of the flat. Did you see it? There it is again. That's the mouth of a surface-feeding carp! There's another and another. It's tough to tell if they broke off from the circulators, but no matter where they came from, cloopers are too precious to waste. What should we do?

   a. Remembering all that we've learned, slowly and quietly move to an intercept position.

b. Wait for the tailers to return.

c. More planning ... again.

Hey, you're getting the idea! Yes, we're going to do some planning, for two reasons. First, those tailers just might return and they are a far more certain target than the cloopers. Second, while we wait, we can make some observations about the cloopers.

They aren't all that far away, so let's check the water around us. Are there bugs coming off or emergers in the film? If there are, we'll match the hatch. If we don't see anything, they're probably clooping midges off the surface ... time for a Griffith's Gnat. Are there, instead, lots of cottonwood or dandelion seeds on the surface? Whatever they're eating, there should be lots of it because it takes a good opportunity to convince carp to feed on the surface with consistency.

If we're committed to taking a crack at the cloopers, it's time to take the sun, the course of the fish, and the cover they'll head for into consideration. There's another, deceptively simple factor to consider at this time. Just how deep is the water where they're feeding, anyway?

One of the things that helps carp feel comfortable enough to cloop is immediate access to deep water in case of trouble. Carp clooping over deep water may eventually work their way into shallow water as long as a wading angler doesn't put them down by blundering around or, worse, by making a wild, double-hauled "Hail Mary" cast to fish that are really out of reach. If they're out of reach, don't push your luck. All things (including, sometimes, carp) come to those who wait.

Oh, yes, while we're waiting, watching, and thinking about our next move, we might also add five or six feet of 5X tippet to our leaders. Just a suggestion. It would be a shame to spook these carp with our leaders when we've waited so long.

Okay, let's try to track them. Tough, isn't it? Brad and I had a terrible time with this until we finally discovered that, although the carp appear to be moving randomly, they're actually traveling on a base course that can be predicted to some degree. On the other hand, sometimes what appear to be random movements are actually random movements. Isn't carp fishing great? Sorry, but you'll just have to do the best you can.

Now, if we're still committed to trying for these fish, what should we do next?

a. Taking into account all the guidelines we used for tailers, begin moving into position to cast to these fish.
b. Wait some more.

Ah-hah! Gotcha! We'll begin moving into position, but just to complicate our lives, we'll add a couple more factors into the equation. First, we must at all times remember that these fish are spooky. Even if we don't put them down, they can simply ease away from us, staying maddeningly just beyond casting range. So, we're going to stalk these fish. Let's be sure not to stumble, feeling each footstep before planting our boots, and to wade as quietly as we can.

Second, to minimize the chances of frightening the fish, we're going to place ourselves the farthest distance from them at which we can cast accurately. This is no time for bravado or bragging. Really, how far can you be from a one-foot square target and expect to hit it? Forty feet? Fine. Sixty feet? Better. Twenty feet? We hope you can wade very quietly!

There is a reason for this small target area. Remember what we said about carp liking lots of food on the surface before they risk clooping? The corollary to this is that, with food present in abundance, the window of a clooping carp is likely to be quite small. We've had carp charge an adult damselfly imitation, but with smaller, less active prey, carp work a restricted area.

Now, you've made your best stab at defining the limits of the shoal, right? Which fish are you going to cast to? Precisely! The one that's trailing and on our side of the main shoal. You won't line any other fish, and if you get lucky and hook it, you just might sneak it out of the shoal without spooking its companions.

What's that? How close should you cast? Well, we're afraid that it's still a bit of a gamble, but there are a couple of things that

The window of a clooping carp is small, so accurate casting is required. (Barry Reynolds)

can load the dice in your favor. Placing you fly much closer than a foot is dangerous in our opinion. Three feet, in our experience, is a bit far for cloopers, except in very clear, very flat water. The water here is a bit cloudy and there is a little chop on the surface. Try for about two feet.

What's the fish doing? Coming closer. Coming closer. What is with that fish? Is it blind? Yep, it missed your fly or ignored it. Now, we're going to leave the fly out and wait again. There's another trailer we didn't notice and it's coming right down on your fly. Okay, we'll make it tougher to miss this time. Give that fly a twitch. You're fishing a seed fly? Hey, carp are smart, but they're not that smart!

The carp took the fly. Go easy. Whoops. I guess we forgot to tell you that when you hook an already-nervous clooper, it will react very quickly. Sorry about your fly and tippet; maybe 5X *was* just a bit light.

The cloopers have all disappeared, so let's look at the water again. What's that over there, in those mucky shallows? It's a patch of muddy water and it's likely to be carp, rooting around in the muck. Time to plan our next move. What now?

a. Move over there.

b. Wait and watch again.

As you might guess, we'll do a bit more watching, but this time, we'll do it as we move. That mud is both a blessing and a curse, you know. It obscures the carp's vision, giving the fish a feeling of security and making mudding carp the least spooky carp you'll cast to. However, it can be very difficult to define the limits of the shoal and find a target fish. In really fine sediments, when carp are feeding very aggressively, just a few carp can create a huge mud.

As we move over there, it's time to consider our choice of flies. Here's what mudding carp are likely to be doing. Their snouts and sensitive barbels are buried in the muck and they're rooting along until they feel, taste, or smell something of interest. When that happens, they inhale a mouthful of the bottom. Then they either vigorously expel the mud, picking out the food items as the mud breaks up or they sieve out the food, expelling the mud through their gills. In either event, sediment and food wind up suspended in the water. With your fly, you're trying to give them something attractive that is easy for the carp to find and catch.

That unweighted 'Bou Face just might do the trick. It will sink slowly and it's got both motion and flash to attract the fish. Now we have to decide where to cast.

We tend to be a bit more casual about mudding carp, breaking some otherwise hard-and-fast rules about approach and presentation. Since we usually can't see individual fish, we cast either where the mud is thickest and most of the fish are or we cast to the front of the mud where the leading carp have the best opportunity to see the fly. In either case, we usually won't have to worry about spooking the fish unless we make a mistake of some kind.

That cast should do nicely—right in the middle of the thickest mud. This is a confusing moment, isn't it? What to do now? First off, give the fly a little time to sink. Next, swim it around a bit, slowly, as if it were a bit of drifting detritus or a surprised nymph. Still nothing? Cast again and watch the end of your line. It's a lot like dead-drift nymph fishing, isn't it? Strike!

Casting to the lead fish in a group of mudders can produce fish like this. (Barry Reynolds)

Hey, that's the biggest one so far! Nice fish! You're right, this is a place where a strike indicator could come in handy, and we do use them from time to time.

You know, it's about time for lunch. Let's sit down and relax, have a sandwich, and talk a bit.

The purpose of this admittedly idealized fishing trip was to combine in one chapter what we've discussed in the preceding seven. We wanted to show you that catching carp on fly tackle is a matter of keeping some relatively simple rules in mind, of being a keen observer, and of thinking things through.

In other words, it's a matter of bringing a bit of book learning together with the skills and commitment that you, as a flyfisher, already have. This is something you do automatically when you cast to any fish. The lesson of this chapter is simple. If you approach carp with the same commitment you bring to other fish, we don't see how you can fail to be successful. We hope the book has made you feel that carp deserve that commitment. The carp themselves will make you certain of it.

———————

You're ready, the carp are waiting. Go get 'em!

DAVE WHITLOCK'S FAVORITE CARP FLIES

I choose my carp flies as carefully as if I were fishing for selective brown trout or spooky permit. It's important to imitate the foods that resident carp are currently feeding on. Size, color, shape, and action are all important.

Carp flies must not scare the fish with a loud splash and must quickly get down to the level carp are feeding. Because of this, I use a lot of aquatic imitations, especially nymphs and spinners or spent adults.

My Red Fox Squirrel Hair Nymph series in the right size and proportions seldom fails me when carp are eating aquatic nymphs and larvae. For really large carp of fifteen to thirty pounds, I've enjoyed consistent results on my NearNuff Crayfish (see page 104 for pattern) and NearNuff Sculpin series. I attribute this to the carp's attraction to live, active, bottom-dwelling crayfish and small fish that these bottom-jigging flies effectively represent.

I've also included the Mulberry Fly for those parts of the country where mulberries fall into creeks each spring. Carp love them.

Dave Whitlock

Red Fox Squirrel Hair Nymph

Hook:	Nymph or streamer, 3XL, e.g., Tiemco TMC 5263, sizes 4-14
Thread:	Orange
Weight:	Lead wire
Tail:	Red fox squirrel back hair
Ribbing:	Gold oval tinsel
Abdomen:	Whitlock/SLF Dubbing—red fox squirrel hair belly
Thorax:	Whitlock/SLF Dubbing—red fox squirrel hair back
Legs:	One turn of speckled brown hen back

(Note: For carp, I tie three variations of this nymph, depending on where the carp are and what they're feeding on. The "regular" version is listed above. The bead-head version adds additional weight and flash. The last version is the bead-head version with pumpkin Silly Legs added for motion and improved visibility.)

Red Fox Squirrel Hair Nymph

Bead-Head version

Rubber-Legged Bead-Head version

Whitlock NearNuff Sculpin

Hook:	Nymph or streamer, 3XL, e.g., Tiemco TMC 5263, sizes 4-10
Thread:	To match color of body
Weight:	Lead wire or Wapsi lead dumbbell eyes
Tail:	Four soft, flexible grizzly body feathers, dyed sculpin's color
Flash:	Four strands of Krystal Flash
Body:	Whitlock/SLF Dubbing—NearNuff Sculpin dubbing, olive or light brown
Body hackle:	Webby grizzly cock hackle, dyed olive or light brown

Whitlock NearNuff Sculpin

Dave's Mulberry Fly

Hook:	Nymph or streamer, 2XL, e.g., Tiemco TMC 5262, sizes 6 and 8
Thread:	Red
Tail:	Light green hackle stem
Body:	Red and purple deer hair

Dave's Mulberry Fly

INDEX

Adult Damselfly, 89
Agent Orange, 99, 117
amur, white, 26
Ant, 92
ants, 58, 66, 67, 92, 113
Back Swimmer, 100
back swimmers, 100
backing, fly line, 128–129
Baird, S. F., 13
baitfish, 3, 31, 55, 56, 73, 102,
       106, 114, 115, 116
barbels, 20, 21, 144
Barr, John, 77, 81
Barr 'Bou Face, 64, 102, 111,
       117, 120, 123, 144
Barr's Bead-Head Fup, 81
Barr's Damselfly Nymph, 77
Barr's Dragonfly Nymph, 78
Bead-Head Prince Nymph, 74,
       117, 139
Bead-Head Stonefly Nymph, 79
bead-heads, 63, 148
beetles, aquatic, 54, 65, 83
  terrestrial, 58, 92, 94
Befus' Epoxy Scud, 101, 117

Befus' Flying Ant, 93
Befus' Parachute Emerger, 86
Befus' Wiggle Bug, 80, 115, 117,
       120, 123
BogaGrip, 130–131
bonefish, 7, 9, 40, 45, 54, 99, 129
Cache La Poudre River, 68
caddisflies, 55, 66, 68
Callibaetis CDC Biot Mayfly,
       87
Callibaetis CDC Biot Spinner,
       88
carp, diet of, 22–23, 29, 53–70
  effects of weather on, 38–39
  feeding habits of, 31–35, 53-54,
       56-61
  flies for, 19, 62, 63, 64, 65, 66,
       70, 71–106, 147–151
  grass, 11, 25–30, 69–70, 75, 90
  habitats of, 17–18, 28
  history of, 11–14, 25–26
  leather, 13, 16, 17
  life span of, 16–17, 27
  mirror, 13, 16, 17
  range of, 15, 26–27

record, 8, 15, 16
reproduction in, 21–22, 28–29,
    114
scaled, 13, 16
selectivity in, 7, 71, 114
senses of, 18–21, 28
stationary, 46–48, 82, 98,
    118–120, 123–124
sunbathing, 45–46, 118, 121,
    123
temperature range of, 17–18
caterpillars, 58
CDC Cottonwood Seed, 91
circulators, 49–51, 117, 138-140
clams, 55, 56, 62
cloopers, 42, 44, 66, 84, 86, 89,
    90, 92, 113–114, 116,
    121–122, 130, 140–143
Clouser Minnow, 57, 105
Clouser Swimming Nymph, 73,
    109, 111, 117
Colorado, 3, 5, 55, 67, 68, 84, 88
crane flies, 64
crayfish, 55, 56, 62, 64, 73, 99,
    102, 104, 109, 111, 137, 147
cressbugs, 55
crickets, 58, 84, 92, 96
crud flies, 65, 68, 70
cruisers, 48–51, 68, 69, 105,
    116–117, 122–123, 137, 138
damselflies, 3, 42, 54, 60, 65, 66,
    67, 73, 77, 84, 89, 109, 114,
    142
damselfly nymph, 77, 109, 111
Dandelion Seed, 90
Dave's Mulberry Fly, 147, 151
dragonflies, 65, 66, 73, 78
duckweed, 65

Elevenmile Reservoir, 3, 67
emergers, 86, 114
feeding window, 136–137, 140
Flaming Gorge Reservoir, 46
flies, dry, 84–91
fly lines, 129
fly reels, 128–129
fly rods, 127
grass carp, 11, 25–30, 69–70, 75,
    90
Griffith's Gnat, 44, 67, 84, 85,
    114
Hare's Ear Nymph, 109, 111,
    120, 124, 136
hell raisers, 114–115, 125
hellgrammites, 64
hook, barbless, 130, 138
hoppers, 42, 58, 68, 84, 92, 96
Koi, 15
leaders, 129–130, 141, 143
leeches, 55, 65, 73, 102
Marabou Clouser Minnow, 105
mayflies, 42, 55, 60, 66, 68, 86,
    87, 88
Midge Larva, 82
midges, 3, 42, 54, 65, 67, 84, 86,
    113, 114, 122, 130
minnows, 64, 102
mollusks, 55, 62
Mr. Twister, 80
mudders, 111–112, 117, 143–145
mussels, 55, 56, 62
nets, 130
No-Name Baitfish, 106, 116
nymphs, 62, 65, 72–83, 102, 109,
    130, 137, 147
open-water fishing, 120–125
Pelahatchie Lake, 16

pharyngeal teeth, 14, 15, 23, 27, 56, 62
pheromones, 20, 24
polliwogs, 65
Poppe, Julius, 14
Prince Nymph, 109, 111, 120, 123
Red Fox Squirrel Hair Nymph, 147, 148, 149
Reynolds' 'Poxy 'Dad, 103
Robinson, Capt. Henry, 14
rooters, 110–111, 116, 117
Rubber-Legged Hare's Ear Nymph, 76
salamanders, 65
San Juan Worm, 83, 109, 111
schreckstoff, 20, 24, 138
scuds, 55, 101, 111, 120, 124
seed flies, 39, 42, 70, 71, 90, 91, 143
seeds, 113
  cattail, 59, 60
  cottonwood, 59, 60, 67, 114
  dandelion, 59, 60, 67
  milkweed, 67
  mulberry, 59, 60
  thistle, 59, 60
shallow-water fishing, 61–66, 74, 108–120, 136
shoaling, 23–25, 30, 39, 136, 139, 142

snails, 55, 56, 62, 66
sowbugs, 55
Stewart's Spider, 97
stoneflies, 64, 79, 109
stripers, 57
sunglasses, polarized, 131, 135
Super Bugger, 81
surface feeding, 19, 41–45, 55, 59, 66, 89, 90, 92, 113, 140–143
tadpoles, 73
tailers, 108–109, 116, 117, 135–136, 139, 140, 141
terrestrials, 58–59, 92–98
Thistle Seed, 90
trash fish, 3, 4, 6
weed guards, 64
Whitlock, Dave, 147
Whitlock Beetle, 94
Whitlock Cricket, 95, 96
Whitlock Hopper, 95
Whitlock NearNuff Crayfish, 104, 147
Whitlock NearNuff Sculpin, 147, 150
Woolly Bugger, 46, 64, 75, 120
Woolly Worm, 59, 97, 98
worms, aquatic, 54, 62, 65, 83
  terrestrial, 58

Other Spring Creek Press Flyfishing Titles

Available from your local bookseller,
fly shop, or Johnson Books.

Beyond Trout: A Flyfishing Guide
Barry Reynolds and John Berryman

Pike on the Fly:
The Flyfishing Guide to Northerns, Tigers, and Muskies
Barry Reynolds and John Berryman

Flyfishing Alaska
Revised Edition
Anthony J. Route

Flies for Alaska:
A Guide to Buying and Tying
Anthony J. Route

Poul Jorgensen's Book of Fly Tying:
A Guide to Flies for All Game Fish
Poul Jorgensen

Woolly Worms and Wombats:
A Sidelong Glance at Flyfishing Down Under
Chris Dawson

An Angler's Guide to Aquatic Insects and Their Imitations
Revised Edition
Rick Hafele and Scott Roederer